P9-CRS-541

Albert Einstein

Albert
Einstein

Frieda Wishinsky

DK Publishing, Inc.

LONDON, NEW YORK, MUNICH,
MELBOURNE, AND DELHI

Editor : Elizabeth Hester
Publishing Director : Beth Sutinis
Art Director : Dirk Kaufman
Creative Director : Tina Vaughan
Designer : Jessica Lasher
Photo Research : Anne Burns Images
Production : Ivor Parker
DTP Designer : Milos Orlovic

First American Edition, 2005

06 07 08 09 10 9 8 7 6 5 4 3
Published in the United States
by DK Publishing, Inc.
375 Hudson St., New York, New York 10014

DK books are available at special discounts for bulk purchases
for sales promotions, premiums, fund-raising, or educational use.
For details, contact:

DK Publishing Special Markets
375 Hudson Street
New York, NY 10014
SpecialSales@dk.com

Published in Great Britain by Dorling Kindersley Limited.

Library of Congress Cataloging-in-Publication Data

Wishinsky, Frieda.
Albert Einstein / by Frieda Wishinsky.-- 1st American ed.
p. cm. -- (DK biography)
Includes index.
ISBN 0-7566-1247-0 (pbk.) -- ISBN 0-7566-1248-9 (plc)
1. Einstein, Albert, 1879-1955. 2. Physicists--Biography--Juvenile literature. I. Title. II. Series.
QC16.E5.W57 2005
530'.092--dc22

2005007006

Color reproduction by GRB Editrice, Italy
Printed and bound in China by
South China Printing Co., Ltd.

Photography credits:
Front cover: Bettmann/CORBIS. Back cover: © Bettmann/CORBIS.
Border Photos (from left to right): Corbis/BettmanCorbis/Hulton-
DeutschGetty Images/Time Life Pictures; Getty/AFP; Corbis/
Sotheby's/ R.Miman/Sygma; Corbis/ Underwood & Underwood;
California Institute of Technology Archives; Corbis/Bettmann;
Corbis/Underwood & Underwood; Corbis/ Bettman; Corbis/Michael
S.Yamashita; California Institute of Technology Archives; Getty
Images/Time Life Pictures.

Discover more at
www.dk.com

Contents

More Than a Clerk

How does light pass through space? Can light, space, and time be defined? What is the relationship between these entities? How do they function? These were the questions that consumed and intrigued Albert Einstein during his long hours as a patent clerk in Bern, Switzerland.

Working at the patent office wasn't the kind of job Albert had dreamed about when he attended the Polytechnic Institute in Switzerland. He wasn't a professor with a horde of admiring students hanging on to his every word. In fact, his own teachers had thought Albert had too much arrogance and attitude—and without their recommendation, his applications to teach physics had been turned down. Instead, he had to sit on a stool for hours checking out patents for toasters or mechanical vegetable peelers.

Arrogance and attitude. People had always complained he had too much of those qualities. Life would have been easier for Albert if he had been more careful with his words and followed the rules. But rules were difficult for him. They'd been difficult for him ever since he was a young boy.

However, Albert enjoyed his job. He liked checking new inventions to see if they were original and workable. And the position gave him time to think—not only about someone else's latest invention, but also about his own scientific ideas. Even though being a patent clerk wasn't a prestigious job, he was grateful to have the work. It helped him support his family, his wife Mileva and his one-year-old son Hans Albert. And he had good friends outside work who loved to spend hours discussing the scientific mysteries that absorbed them all.

All his life, Albert had tried to answer questions about the natural world that most people would consider unanswerable. But this year, 1905, would be the year of his big breakthroughs. As he told a friend, "A storm broke loose in my mind." After countless hours of thought and analysis, some of the answers to his scientific questions came to him. That year, Albert carefully described his findings in five scientific papers and sent them off for publication.

All he had to do now was wait. But waiting was hard. How would his paper be received in the scientific community? Would professional scientists take him seriously? After all, he didn't even have an advanced degree. He was still just a 26-year-old unknown scientist working in a patent office.

1

When Albert Was a Boy

Albert Einstein came from a family of merchants, skilled workers, and shopkeepers who had lived in small towns and villages in southwest Germany for many years. Hermann and Pauline Einstein lived in Ulm, Germany, a small city on the Danube River with narrow, winding streets and a skyline dominated by Ulm Cathedral. Hermann was a good-natured, optimistic man who loved outings in the countryside. He was also a businessman, but for most of his life his businesses were unsuccessful. Pauline was an accomplished musician who enjoyed literature. She liked to play the piano and especially appreciated the music of the renowned German composer Ludwig van Beethoven. Hermann and Pauline were a close and happy couple.

The Einsteins were Jewish, but they weren't particularly religious. They didn't follow the strict Jewish dietary laws, rituals, and customs that some families observed. And though there were some clear divisions between Jewish and German culture at this time, Pauline and Hermann enjoyed German literature

Albert's parents, Hermann and Pauline, were married on August 8, 1876.

Pauline and Hermann Einstein were a close and devoted couple. Albert was their first child.

and music and fit in comfortably with their Christian neighbors.

On March 14, 1879, Pauline gave birth to the Einstein's first child, Albert. From the day he was born, Albert was unusual. He had a large, misshapen head and a big body. When his grandmother Jette saw him for the first time, she screamed, "Much too fat! Much too fat!" Albert's concerned parents consulted doctors who assured them that in time, Albert would look normal. Over time, his head straightened out, but Albert's behavior baffled and worried the family.

For one thing, Albert was slow to speak. His parents feared that he was mentally disabled. When he finally did begin to speak, it was carefully and not very often. Years later, Albert himself recalled, "When I was between two and

Albert Einstein was born in this building in Ulm, Germany, and lived there with his family for about a year.

three, I formed the ambition to speak in whole sentences. I would try each sentence out on myself by saying it softly. Then when it seemed right, I would say it out loud."

Once Albert learned to speak, he began asking startling questions. When he was three, he thought his new baby sister, Maja, was a toy. When he first saw her he asked, "Where are the wheels?"

Albert's fierce temper tantrums were also a concern. His sister Maja recalled that when he was in the throes of a tantrum, "his face would turn pale and the tip of his nose would become white and he would lose control of himself."

By the time Maja was born, the family was living in Munich, the big, bustling capital of southern Germany. In Ulm, Hermann Einstein's small electric and engineering business hadn't done well. Hermann's younger brother,

Electric power

Electricity is the force that makes lightning flash with frightening power. In the 19th century scientists and engineers were beginning to use electricity to power new inventions like the telephone and to light cities. Thomas Edison's invention of the lightbulb in the late 1800s accelerated the use of electricity to power homes and industry, but it was still new to many towns when Albert was a child. In 1883, four-year-old Albert watched as the first building in Munich was lit by electric power.

Jakob, who was a trained engineer, proposed that they move to Munich to start an electrochemical business there together. Munich was growing

and had more opportunities than a small backwater town like Ulm. Hermann and Jakob borrowed money from Pauline Einstein's well-to-do family, rented a small house for the family to live in, and began their business. They decided that Hermann would be in charge of sales, and Jakob would be the technical expert.

After a few years, Jakob suggested they expand their company and produce electric generators and other equipment to provide electricity and power lighting systems. Jakob, who had received patents for a number of his inventions, wanted to use some of them in the business. Soon the Einstein business began to thrive. The brothers hosted an exhibit at Munich's International Electric Exhibition in 1882. In 1885, they were awarded a contract to provide the first electric lighting to the Bavarian Oktoberfest, a huge annual German folk festival. By this time, the Einsteins had two hundred

> *"I would try each sentence out on myself.... Then, when it seemed right, I would say it out loud."*
>
> —Albert Einstein on his slow speech as a child

11

employees. Soon they were supplying power stations in Italy as well as Germany. After five years in Munich, Albert's family was doing well enough to move to Sendling, a suburb of Munich, where they settled into a pleasant stone house surrounded by trees and a large garden. Jakob and his wife, Ida, moved into the attached house next door and shared a garden with the Einsteins.

While Hermann and Jakob were at work, Pauline was busy at home taking care of the two children. She was a stern but loving mother. She didn't pamper her children but encouraged them to be independent. She even let Albert walk around the neighborhood streets by himself, although she kept a watchful eye on him. She also encouraged the children's musical education. Maja

Albert enjoyed his sister Maja's company and rarely played with other children.

"Where are the wheels?"

—Albert Einstein's first reaction to his baby sister, Maja

took piano lessons, and Albert took violin lessons. But Albert found the violin classes uninspiring and uninteresting. He hated being forced to practice. One day, in a rage, he even threw a chair at his teacher. Nevertheless, Albert's mother, who was used to his temper tantrums, was determined that Albert was going to learn to play the violin. She found him another, stricter teacher, and Albert reluctantly proceeded with his lessons.

Albert was a loner and rarely played with other children besides Maja. Even when the children of relatives visited, and Maja would run and jump with them in the garden, Albert kept to himself. He didn't like the rough, active games that other children played, or pretending to march like soldiers.

Although Albert got along well with his sister most of the time, sometimes his temper would erupt. Maja was usually able to run for cover before he exploded, but once when

As a young boy Albert hated playing the violin, but later in life it would become one of his favorite ways to relax.

13

she didn't get out of his way quickly enough, Albert hit her over the head with a garden hoe. She was angry at the time but later grew to understand Albert's tantrums. Years later she laughingly said, "A sound skull is needed to be the sister of a thinker."

Gradually Albert's temper subsided, and he found other things to engage his interest. Although he didn't like physical exercise, he enjoyed playing with a small boat, which he sailed in a pail of water. He liked toys with wheels and moving parts. He had a passion for puzzles, for building structures out of blocks, and for erecting towers out of cards. Building a tower of thin cards takes patience and a steady hand. Albert once painstakingly built one 14 stories high, and proudly showed it to his family before it collapsed. Maja tried building a tall tower out of cards, too, but could only make it reach four stories before it fell down.

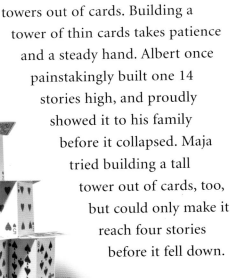

Albert became adept at building tall towers out of cards.

When Albert was five years old and sick in bed, his father brought him a compass to keep him amused while he recuperated. Albert was fascinated and intrigued by the compass. He spun it and shook it and rattled it—but no matter what he did, the needle always pointed north. He wondered what invisible force made the needle always point in the

A compass is an instrument for determining direction. It uses a magnetized needle or group of needles that turn freely on a pivot and point to the earth's magnetic north.

same direction. He could tell that some powerful force was responsible for this behavior and wanted to figure out what it was. Little did he know, that's just the sort of work he would be doing all his life. When he was older, he said he never forgot that compass. "I can still remember—or at least I believe I can remember—that this experience made a deep and abiding impression on me," he said. Albert believed that his fascination with the compass inspired his passion for science.

> *"A sound skull is needed to be the sister of a thinker."*
>
> —Maja Einstein

2

School

Albert was tutored at home until he was six years old. When it was time for him to begin formal school, he was sent to the local Catholic school, which was the closest school to his house. Germany had a history of religious persecution—one hundred years earlier, Jews had been forced to live separately from the rest of the population in areas called ghettos. Even though some prejudice remained, the 1880s were a much more peaceful time. Although Albert was the only Jewish child in the class, having a different religious background wasn't an obstacle for him. What he disliked about school was sitting still for hours, following strict rules, and memorizing. The German school system didn't encourage students to discuss or debate ideas.

Albert's teachers thought he was inattentive

Jews in Germany

Jews have lived in Germany for more than 1,500 years. There have been periods when Jews lived comfortably amid their Christian neighbors, but at other times anti-Jewish feeling rose and led to violence. Although the mid-1800s was a period of relative calm for Jews in Germany, as the new century approached, there was again renewed anti-Semitism. Eventually, with the rise of the Nazis in the 1930s, anti-Jewish sentiment erupted into the state-ordered murder of German Jews.

and a daydreamer. They complained that he spoke slowly and hesitantly and had a habit of repeating his thoughts to himself after voicing them aloud. They noted that he had trouble

A rap across the knuckles with a ruler like this one was a common punishment in stern German classrooms.

remembering facts. It was true. Albert tried hard to adapt, for he hated having his knuckles hit with a ruler or stick, one of the punishments for misbehavior at school. But he wasn't always successful. He thought the teachers in the elementary school were like sergeants in the army.

Albert didn't make many friends at school. He was quiet and withdrawn and was often alone. His classmates often teased him for keeping to himself. He didn't enjoy sports as many of the other boys did, and he disliked playing soldiers, a passionate pastime for his schoolmates. When he watched soldiers in a military parade marching through the streets of Munich, he cringed, while others cheered and applauded. He saw marching as a coercive activity, where people were compelled to blindly follow a leader. He never wanted to be a soldier as so many other boys dreamed of becoming when they grew up.

Despite Albert's daydreaming, he still excelled in much of

"Albert was again at the top of his class."

—Pauline Einstein

his schoolwork. In 1886, his mother wrote: "Albert got his grades yesterday, he was again at the top of his class; he brought home a brilliant record." Albert always did well in subjects that engaged him, such as math and Latin. He liked the logic and clarity of those subjects but found other subjects, like French, more difficult.

Albert was ten when he attended the Luitpold-Gymnasium. It was a large school by German standards

with more than one thousand students. Only five percent of the students were Jewish, and the rest were Catholic. Here, too, Albert had few friends. The students thought he was a dreamer. They called him a "Biedermeier," which meant "honest John," because he was so conscientious and careful about never making a false statement. At the gymnasium, he studied Latin, Greek, German, French, math, and science. He disliked Greek and most languages except Latin but, as always, did well in science and math. As in his elementary school, Albert felt that the atmosphere at the gymnasium was too regimented. Except for his literature professor, Herr Reuss, he felt most of the teachers didn't encourage students to think for themselves, and the rigid tone of the school didn't inspire Albert to love learning. He later said: "The worst thing seems to be for a school principally to work with methods of fear, force and artificial authority. Such treatment destroys healthy feelings, the integrity and self-confidence of the pupils."

Many of the teachers at the gymnasium weren't impressed with Albert either. They disliked his disinterested attitude and said that

Albert is the only student smiling in this group picture from his school days in Munich. He's the third child from the right in the front row.

Algebra is a branch of mathematics that uses symbols and numbers to show mathematical relationships.

it had a negative impact on his performance. When Hermann Einstein asked one of Albert's teachers what profession his son should pursue, the professor said it didn't matter, because Albert was unlikely to excel in anything.

Luckily there were two people in Albert's life who changed his feeling about learning, although neither of them were his teachers at school. His uncle Jakob, who lived near the Einsteins and was an inventor and engineer, inspired Albert to love algebra. Uncle Jakob turned algebra into a game by referring to X as a little animal that was unknown. "When we bag our animal, we pounce on it and give it the right name," he told Albert. Albert loved the playfulness and challenge of Uncle Jakob's game. Maja reported that Albert would never give up until he could solve a problem, and then he would jump for joy. "Persistence and tenacity were already part of his character and would become more prominent," Maja wrote years later. The other person who influenced Albert's love of math, science, and philosophy was a 21-year-old medical student named Max Talmud who attended Munich University. It was a tradition in many Jewish households that a student would be invited regularly for supper. Max Talmud (later known as Max Talmey), visited the Einsteins on Thursdays.

"In all those years, I never saw him reading any light literature."

—Max Talmud on Albert's taste in books

Although Max and Albert were 10 years apart in age, they became friends and spent hours talking. Max described the Einstein household as "happy, comfortable and cheerful" and felt he was warmly welcomed by the family.

Max knew Albert was interested in science. "In all those years," Max later said, "I never saw him reading any light literature. Nor did I see him in the company of schoolmates or other boys of his own age." Max introduced Albert to popular scientific books. Max wrote: "He showed a particular inclination toward physics and took pleasure in conversing on physical phenomenon. I gave him therefore for reading matter A. Bernstein's

Medical student Max Talmud provided Albert with science books. The two loved talking about science, philosophy, and books.

Popular Books on Physical Science and L. Buchner's *Force and Matter*, two works that were then quite popular in Germany. The boy was profoundly impressed by them." Albert was particularly inspired by Bernstein, whose descriptions of the physical forces at work in the world he found clear and engaging.

The books Max gave Albert covered a wide range of subjects, including animals, plants, meteors, volcanoes, and climate. They helped Albert formulate questions about the universe and encouraged him to think in new ways. Max wrote that Albert read these books with "breathless suspense."

Geometry fascinated Albert. He loved examining the figures and physical problems it presented.

When he was 11, Albert was instructed about Judaism

by a distant relative
to fulfill the state's
requirement that children
be taught about their
religion. For a year he was

intensely interested in religion. He wanted to become kosher, which meant following strict Jewish dietary laws. He even composed several songs in honor of God, which he'd enthusiastically sing to himself on the way home from school. But a year later, as he grew more interested in science, he became less enthusiastic about religion and its practices. He still enjoyed reading the *Proverbs of Solomon* and the Bible, and continued to be attracted to the ethical values in biblical texts. His interest in ethics and values led

him to read philosophers and writers like Friedrich Schiller and Johann Wolfgang von Goethe. He appreciated their views that stressed the creative powers of the individual and agreed with their dislike of authoritarian societies that didn't value individual achievement.

During the summer when Albert was 12 years old, he received the geometry book his class would be using the next year at school. He loved the book and couldn't wait to begin working through the exercises and sharing them with Max. It was fun figuring out proofs for geometric theorems, and Albert did every one in the book on his own before the school year even began. He thought the logic, harmony, and straightforwardness of geometry were wonderful. Albert later called this book his "Holy Geometry book." Albert also began to teach himself higher mathematics from books, and Max declared, "Soon the flight of his mathematical genius was so high that I could no longer follow." But even when they didn't discuss math, Max and Albert continued to talk about other subjects like philosophy, and Albert continued to impress Max with his ability at age 13 to grasp concepts that confused even grown men and women.

At this time, Albert also became enthralled with the music of composer Wolfgang Amadeus Mozart. Suddenly his whole attitude toward music changed. He wanted to play the violin, the instrument he'd so violently resisted as a child. He was so excited by music, he couldn't wait to practice and try out new tunes. Maja recalled that he "constantly searched for new harmonies of his own invention." He even began playing duets with his mother.

"Love is a better teacher than a sense of duty."

—Albert Einstein

He later wrote: "I believe on the whole that love is a better teacher than a sense of duty—with me, at least, it certainly was." He found that music could even help him mull over difficult studies; he would sometimes stop his practice suddenly, leap up, and cry, "There, now, I've got it." While practicing, his mind was also working on his scientific and mathematical ideas. Albert appreciated the logical structure of Mozart's sonatas. He felt they resembled mathematics in their composition.

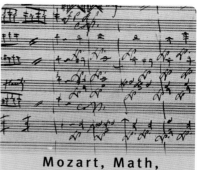

Mozart, Math, and Einstein

Wolfgang Amadeus Mozart (1756–1791) was a brilliant musician and composer. He began playing keyboard at the age of three and composed small pieces by the age of five, symphonies by nine, and operas by twelve. Mozart also loved math and puzzles, and, like Einstein, was intense and passionate about his work. Some studies have suggested that the logical, mathematical form of Mozart's sonatas can help people learn more effectively.

Learning was becoming exciting for Albert, but school was not.

3

In Trouble

When Albert was 15, his family's business ran into trouble again. Despite Jakob's new inventions for electric meters and generators, the Einstein brothers faced tough competition from other firms that were bigger and had more money to invest. The Einsteins tried to raise the funds they needed, but they couldn't raise enough. Eventually, the business collapsed. The family didn't know what to do. Luckily, Pauline's relatives came to the rescue, and so did the Einsteins' Italian business associate, Signor Garrone. Pauline's family and Signor Garrone backed Hermann and Jakob in a new venture installing electricity in Milan, Italy. The family would have to move.

Selling off the business and moving away from home was difficult for everyone, but it was devastating for Albert. The family decided that instead of moving with them, Albert would stay behind in Munich to finish school. He had to leave the spacious family home he loved and move alone into a boarding house. He missed the

As a teenager, Albert couldn't wait to leave his German school.

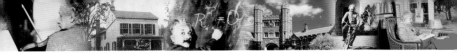

BOARDING HOUSE

A boarding house is a lodging where meals are provided and people can live or "board" for an extended period of time.

company and comfort of his mother, father, Maja, and Uncle Jakob, all of whom had supported him through school. Albert had few friends in Munich. His classmates continued to find him strange and solitary, and his teachers thought he was restless and uncooperative.

At first, Albert put up a brave front, writing short, cheerful letters to his family in Italy. But soon he was so unhappy, he wanted to leave Germany right away. He knew that after age 16 every German boy not attending school was required to go into the army. After his 17th birthday, Albert would not even be allowed to leave Germany until he fulfilled his military obligation. Albert had always hated war and guns; joining the military was the last thing he wanted to do.

The Einsteins' letters about the beauty of Italy only made separation harder on Albert.

As Albert read his family's letters with their glowing descriptions of the beauty of Italy and the friendliness of the people, he wanted to leave Germany even more. He knew he had to find a way. It was hard making such a big decision on his own, but he felt he had no choice but to act. Albert spoke to his doctor, Bernard Talmud, an older brother of his friend Max, about his troubles at school. Dr. Talmud agreed to write a note stating that Albert was on the verge of a nervous breakdown and needed rest. Albert also approached his mathematics professor, Joseph Ducrue, to write a letter noting that Albert's work in mathematics was ahead of the requirements for graduation. Ducrue sympathized with Albert's situation and agreed to write the letter.

But before Albert could present Dr. Talmud's letter to the school authorities, he was hauled into the office of his Greek professor, Herr Degenhart. Degenhart thought Albert showed a disdainful attitude in class. When Albert protested that he'd done nothing wrong, Degenhart said: "You sit there in the back row smiling. And that undermines the respect a teacher needs from his class." He suggested Albert leave the gymnasium.

Albert loved the beauty of the Italian countryside.

THE ALPS

The Alps are a chain of mountains in south-central Europe that extend from the Mediterranean coast to the west Balkan Peninsula.

Finally, Albert was able to leave the school. He didn't want to stay in Germany a day longer. On December 29, 1894, a few months before his 16th birthday, he packed his belongings and went to the Munich railroad station. The moment the train left Germany, Albert felt freer and happier. As he looked out the window at the beautiful Italian countryside, he couldn't wait to start his life in a new land and be reunited with his family.

Despite their surprise at seeing him and hearing what had happened, Albert's family accepted his decision, especially when he promised that he would soon return to school. Meanwhile, he helped out in the Einsteins' new business. He also read, wrote essays, and traveled around the Italian countryside. Albert loved the

Albert may have taken a train like this in his travels to Italy.

warmth and colors of Italy. He loved hiking in the mountains of the Alps, visiting museums, and meeting the Italian people. He later said, "The people of northern Italy are the most civilized I have ever met." Albert never wanted to return to Germany.

His father encouraged him to train for a practical, sensible career like electric engineering, but Albert knew that wasn't what he wanted to do. He also knew that without further education, it would be hard to find a job. Albert decided that he'd apply for the Swiss Federal Polytechnic Institute in Zurich, Switzerland, a new kind of college devoted to training teachers. All he had to do was pass the entrance exam and he'd be accepted. He was two years younger than most applicants, so he had to receive special permission to take the exam. The test consisted of two parts: a science section and a general information section. Albert studied for both, but he concentrated on the subjects he loved—physics and mathematics—and barely touched on the other subjects such as botany, language, and history, which interested him less.

The exams began on October 8, 1895. On October 24, Albert and his mother were called into the office of Albin Herzog, the director. Herzog told them that Albert had excelled in the mathematical part of the exam but failed the general information section. Albert would not be admitted to the school. Herzog suggested that Albert continue his studies in a Swiss high school and then reapply to the Polytechnic after passing their final exams, called the matura exams.

Although Albert was disappointed, he followed the director's advice. He enrolled in a German-speaking school in the small Swiss town of Aarau, where he could study in his own language. There he would board with the Winteler family. Albert took the train to Aarau, and as soon as he approached his destination, he was delighted to see beautiful forests, meadows, and vineyards. He later described Aarau as "an unforgettable oasis in that European oasis, Switzerland."

Albert liked the Winteler family immediately. Jost Winteler was a history teacher at the Aarau school and he and his family treated Albert with warmth and kindness. Albert enjoyed discussing political issues with the family. They were always tolerant and responsive to different points of view. He joined the family on hikes through the beautiful Swiss countryside. He also spent a lot of of time with one of the Winteler girls, Maria. Although Maria was two years older than Albert, they both loved music and walking and found much to talk about and share.

To his delight, Albert also found the school in Aarau different from the schools in Germany. The atmosphere in Aarau was relaxed, and the teachers were encouraging. Students could even devise their own chemistry experiments— as long as they weren't dangerous.

Albert appreciated the easygoing atmosphere in the Aarau school. In this picture, he is the first student on the left in the front row.

Albert worked hard at improving his knowledge of languages and history. Years later he would remember the school fondly: "This school has left an indelible impression on me because of its liberal spirit and the unaffected thoughtfulness of the teachers, who in no way relied on external authority."

Gradually, Albert's grades improved, and he did well in all his schoolwork at Aarau except for French. But it was in French class, in an essay he titled "Mes Projects d'avenir" ("My Plans for the Future"), that he declared his career objectives. He had decided that he wanted to become a science teacher. He also noted that he loved studying abstract ideas rather than working on practical subjects. He wrote, "My desires have also inspired in me the same resolve. That is quite natural; one always likes to do the things for which one has ability."

Around this time, Albert also began to use his "thought experiments," a way Albert had of picturing a physics problem in his mind. He imagined, for instance, what it would be like to travel alongside a light beam to help him understand how light travels. These "thought experiments" helped Albert formulate his scientific theories.

Albert was also becoming more confident socially.

> *"One always likes to do the things for which one has ability."*
>
> —Albert Einstein

CITIZENSHIP

Citizenship is the legal relationship between an individual and a state. The individual promises loyalty in exchange for the state's protection.

He enjoyed socializing and sought out friends. Although he sometimes had a sarcastic wit, he could also be friendly and charming. One of his classmates, Hans Byland, described Albert as "sure of himself....Nothing escaped his sharp eyes.... Unhampered by convention, his attitude toward the world was that of a laughing philosopher."

Albert was so happy in Italy and Switzerland that he never wanted to return to Germany. His anti-German feelings were so strong, he decided to formally renounce his German citizenship. His father agreed to help him and wrote a letter to the German authorities. On January 28, 1896, Albert's request was granted. He was no longer a German citizen. However, he wasn't a citizen of any country since he was too young to apply for Swiss citizenship.

Although he wasn't a citizen, Albert could apply again for the Swiss Polytechnic Institute. All he had to do was pass the final matura exams.

As a young man, Albert began to make friends. He enjoyed long hikes and long conversations.

chapter 4

The Polytechnic

In September 1896, Albert passed his matura exams. He scored higher than any of the 10 students taking the exams. He now had the academic background he needed to enter the Swiss Polytechnic Institute, but Albert didn't know how he was going to pay the tuition fees. His father's business had failed again, and there was no money for school. The family decided to ask a wealthy aunt for help. Although Albert had never cared for this aunt, whom he thought pompous and vain, he gratefully accepted her help. She agreed to send him a small allowance every month and to pay his tuition.

Albert began the Swiss Polytechnic in October. He was 17 1/2 years old, younger than most of his classmates. He focused

Albert studied mathematics and physics at the Swiss Polytechnic Institute in Zurich. He began his studies at the age of 17 and graduated four years later.

his studies on physics but would also take mathematics and astronomy classes.

Soon Albert made friends with the four other students in his class. One of the students, Marcel Grossmann, liked Albert immediately and recognized his unusual intelligence and potential. "Einstein will be a great man one day," he told his father. Albert's love of music drew him to other friends, and he began attending musical get-togethers where people gathered to listen and play. At one of these events, he met Michele Besso, a mechanical engineer, who for many years became a sounding board for Albert's ideas in physics.

Albert lived in a boarding house and ate at inexpensive cafés or restaurants. His school life was busy, although he often cut classes to study on his own. He listened and played music, spent hours with friends talking about physics and philosophy, sailed, read, and hiked around the beautiful Zurich countryside. Soon he was spending a lot of time with the only female student in the class, Mileva Maric. Mileva was the daughter of a Serbian family who lived in southern Hungary. She had been determined to enter the Swiss Polytechnic Institute and worked diligently to make that happen. Mileva had been born with a hip deformity that made her self-conscious and shy. Still, Albert liked her and found they shared many interests. Although Mileva could be sullen and serious-minded, she loved playing the piano and singing. She helped Albert become more organized and reminded him about tasks or items he forgot. Albert was often absentminded, especially when he was thinking about science. He once told a friend: "When I was a very young man I visited overnight at the home of friends. In the morning I left, forgetting my valise. My host said to my parents: 'That young man will never amount to anything because he can't remember anything.'"

Albert studied for his second-year exams, but since he often skipped classes, his notes were incomplete. Luckily, his loyal friend, Marcel Grossmann, a more careful student, agreed to share his notes. Studying hard and reading Marcel's notes paid off, and Albert passed his exams with high marks.

Now that he'd passed, Albert was ready to proceed to the third year at the Polytechnic. But again, he only attended

The mountains of the Swiss Alps were one of Albert's favorite places to hike.

classes he enjoyed, such as Professor Weber's physics laboratory, and skipped the classes, like Professor Pernet's physics class, that he felt were useless. Albert showed disdain for the professors whose work he didn't respect. His negative attitude infuriated them. He dismissed many of his mathematics classes as unimportant to his understanding of physics and found the mathematics class taught by prominent Professor Hermann Minkowski uninspiring. Minkowski wasn't

Professor Hermann Minkowski, an esteemed mathematician, was one of Albert's teachers at the Swiss Polytechnic. Years later, he strongly supported Albert's theories.

impressed with Albert either and called him a "lazy dog." Years later, Albert would recognize that he had not taken advantage of mathematics at school and that the classes he skipped could have been useful to an understanding of physics. It gradually dawned on him that to truly grasp physics, one had to understand "the most intricate mathematical methods."

Professor Pernet, in particular, was incensed by Albert's behavior. He told Albert: "You are enthusiastic but hopeless at physics. For your own good you should switch to something else." Professor Pernet gave Albert the only failing grade he received at the Polytechnic. Albert received the highest grades from Professor Weber, his physics laboratory professor.

Heinrich Friedrich Weber was one of Albert's professors at the Swiss Polytechnic Institute. At first, Albert enjoyed his classes but eventually lost interest in Weber's outdated theories.

However, Albert was eventually disillusioned even with Professor Weber. He was disappointed that Professor Weber did not let him conduct an experiment on the earth's movement and didn't discuss new theories in physics but stuck with older ideas. Professor Weber resented that Albert insisted on calling him "Herr Weber" instead of the more formal "Professor Weber." Soon Albert started avoiding his class, too, and spent more time studying on his own. He also spent more time with Mileva.

Albert's mother disliked his new girlfriend. She told Albert repeatedly how unhappy his relationship with Mileva made her and how distrustful she was of Mileva. Despite his mother's attitude, Albert continued to see Mileva. Pauline Einstein's opposition became more intense and occasionally she even cried that Mileva would ruin Albert's life and future.

Despite his mother's disapproval, Albert and

THESIS

A thesis is a research paper that presents original research on an academic subject. It is often a requirement for a degree.

Mileva began discussing marriage, which only further angered Pauline. Pauline made her displeasure known to Mileva, who was crushed by her future mother-in-law's cutting remarks.

"Amid all this turmoil, Albert and Mileva continued their studies at the Polytechnic Institute. They prepared for their final exams, and each of them worked on a thesis, a requirement for graduation. When exams were held, Albert passed, but not with the high grades he had achieved in the second- year exams. Nevertheless after having passed the final exams, he could think about job opportunities or further study. He was now qualified to teach math and science in secondary school or perhaps become an assistant to one of his Polytechnic teachers. He also hoped to continue his work in physics and earn a Ph.D., or doctorate degree, which he could pursue at the nearby Zurich University.

But Mileva heard different news about her exams. She'd failed. It was a terrible blow. Nothing seemed to be going right for her. Not only did her future mother-in-law dislike her, but her career in science was possibly over.

"You are enthusiastic but hopeless at physics."

—Professor Pernet, on Einstein's prospects as a scientist

chapter 5

Looking for Work

A lbert was now 21 and a graduate of a fine science institute, but before he could look for work, he needed to become a Swiss citizen. It wasn't an easy process. The application required him to answer personal questions such as: Do you live a respectable life? Do you drink liquor? An investigator checked his record, his job prospects, his family's economic status, and his political beliefs. The investigator saw that Albert's father had little income and felt that so far Albert had little likelihood of employment. Albert wanted to convince the authorities otherwise. There was still a chance when he was called to meet the eight-man Swiss citizenship committee on December 14, 1900. Albert knew he had to persuade the committe that he would make a good, hardworking, and honorable citizen. He had to show them that he was no threat to Switzerland and that he was not a radical thinker. Somehow he managed to do that.

Despite their initial negative report, the

Einstein's citizenship papers allowed him to call Switzerland his home.

committee decided that Albert was "harmless and innocent" and approved his application for citizenship. Albert was delighted.

But there was still another hurdle to overcome. As soon as his Swiss citizenship papers came through, Albert had to report for a medical exam for military service. Every young, healthy man in

The Swiss Military

All able-bodied Swiss men were required by law to spend time in the Swiss military. The Swiss military system is still in place today, although Switzerland has not fought in a war for five hundred years. Women are not required to serve in the army. Every Swiss soldier is issued a Swiss army knife, a multifunctional tool that has also become a favorite of Arctic explorers and mountain climbers.

Switzerland was required to serve in the military. Albert didn't want to join any army, even the Swiss army. Luckily, the doctors discovered that he had flat feet and swollen veins in his legs, and rejected him for service.

Albert was finally free to look for a job. He immediately applied for a position at the Polytechnic Institute. Most of his friends and fellow graduates had found teaching jobs already, some even at the Polytechnic, so he was hopeful that he, too, would be successful. But Albert was rejected for every job. His professors at the Polytechnic could not forget or forgive his attitude toward them when he attended school, and they refused to recommend him for a position. Even Professor Weber, who had first championed Albert, had become so infuriated with him that Albert was sure he wrote a negative

Einstein's friendship with Marcel Grossmann became one of the most important of his life.

reference. He once told Albert: "You're a clever fellow Einstein, but you have one fault. You won't let anyone tell you a thing."

Albert was dejected. He was 22, had few job prospects, and was rapidly running out of money. His father's business was bankrupt again, so he couldn't receive any financial help from his family. And he was still planning to marry Mileva. His one refuge from worry was to work on scientific theories. He could always shut everything else out and think about those problems. So despite his worries, he continued to study and write down his ideas.

Just when he despaired of ever finding work, his friend Marcel Grossmann came to his rescue again. Marcel persuaded his father to recommend Albert to Frederic Haller, director of the Swiss patent office in Bern. As Albert waited to hear from the patent office, he found a temporary job teaching mathematics. Maybe his luck was finally changing.

Albert's family was still opposed to his relationship with Mileva, but he was determined that they would be married soon. And now with the possibility of a real job, he felt more optimistic. So Albert and Mileva decided to take a holiday in the Lake Como area of Switzerland. Lake Como was a beautiful region of mountains and lakes, and the couple enjoyed their time there. But when the holiday was over, Mileva discovered she was pregnant. She knew that neither the Einsteins nor her family would be pleased with the news. She also learned that she had failed the final exam for the Polytechnic a second time. Depressed and worried about her future, Mileva returned to her family's home in Hungary, and Albert and Mileva decided to say nothing to the Einsteins about the baby.

Instead, Albert stayed in Switzerland and buried himself in his scientific work. While still waiting to hear from the patent office about a job, he took on another temporary teaching position. This time he helped prepare an English student at a private school for the high school matura exam. The pay was

Lake Como is a lovely lake region in southern Switzerland. Albert and Mileva, like many other couples, enjoyed the mountain and water views.

modest, but Albert was given room and board at the school. He could also work on his Ph.D. dissertation, which he'd begun under the supervision of Professor Alfred Kleiner from the University of Zurich. He was writing his paper on thermodynamics, the study of heat and its behavior.

In 1902, Albert and Mileva's daughter Lieserl was born. Soon after Lieserl's birth, Albert left his tutoring job. He had a disagreement with the school authorities, who had come to regard him as a bad influence. Everything seemed to be going wrong again. He was a new father with no job or income. And his dissertation had been rejected. Professor Kleiner thought Albert's criticisms of accepted scientific theories were too radical and suggested that Albert withdraw his paper as it was then written. Albert was crushed. All that work and thought, and he would have to redo everything. The only bright spot was the hope of a job at the Bern patent office, but that still hadn't come through. And anyway, would they want to hire him? After all, he'd only been a Swiss citizen for a little over a year, he had difficulties with his professors at school, and his job record was shaky at best.

Albert moved into a small one-room apartment in a rooming house in Bern. He liked Bern and felt comfortable living there. It was a beautiful old Swiss city, encircled by the Aare River, and the Alps were visible in the distance. As Albert waited for his interview for the patent office, he wrote a newspaper ad offering his services as a tutor—

Lieserl Einstein

Mileva wrote Albert when Lieserl was born, and he wrote back that he was happy that he had a daughter. In 1903, Mileva wrote again about Lieserl. That was the last time Lieserl was mentioned in any of the surviving Einstein letters. Albert probably never saw his daughter. Some people have speculated that Lieserl was put up for adoption because Albert and Mileva had no money to care for her. Others think she died. Lieserl's existence was such a secret that few people even knew about her until after both Albert and Mileva died. What happened to Lieserl remains a mystery to this day.

he needed all the paying work he could get. The ad read: "Private lessons in Mathematics and Physics for students and pupils given most thoroughly by Albert Einstein, holder of the fed. polyt. teacher's diploma Gerechtkeitsgasse 32, 1st floor Trial lesson free."

Soon Albert had two students, Maurice Solovine and Conrad Habicht. Albert liked spending time with them, and soon all three men became good friends. They spent hours in cafés or on hikes in the mountains discussing physics and philosophy.

Maurice found Albert an inspiring and patient tutor. "He explained things in a slow and even voice, but in a remarkably clear way."

And then suddenly Albert's luck changed. He was called in to the patent office for an intensive two-hour interview with Frederic Haller, the director. Haller was impressed with Albert's quick understanding and willingness to learn, and Albert was offered the position of technical expert third class. Albert Einstein finally had a real job.

6

A New Start

Albert began work at the Bern patent office on June 23, 1902. The patent office was in a limestone building a few blocks away from the railroad station. At the office, workers sat at tables along the wall under hanging electric lamps and examined applications for patents for new inventions. Before granting a patent, the office had to review descriptions of how the invention was to be used and how it worked. Albert saw proposals for typewriters, cameras, and assorted electric devices. He learned how to read and understand technical drawings.

Director Haller showed him how to analyze an invention, how to determine if there was another similar invention available, and how to decide whether the invention was useful. If the invention passed all these criteria, a patent was issued to the inventor. Albert became adept

Albert looks at a reference book in the patent office.

at simplifying the inventors' often convoluted explanations into short, clear sentences. Working at the patent office taught him how to present his ideas clearly and succinctly. Albert did well at his job and enjoyed the challenge. He also managed to find time to pursue his own scientific ideas in free moments. He said that the job "gave me the opportunity to think about physics."

The patent office was only a few blocks away from his apartment, so every workday, six days a week, Albert walked to his job. Then for the next eight hours, he and the other examiners read patent proposals. At midday, Albert often

The Bern patent office was a large, impressive building.

Albert and his friends Maurice Solovine and Conrad Habicht met regularly to discuss science and philosophy. They called their group the "Olympia Academy."

walked to a dark, cave-like restaurant called Café Bollwerk and ate lunch with his friends Maurice Solovine and Conrad Habicht. They talked for hours about science and philosophy, and dubbed their small group the "Olympia Academy."

In the evenings and on his day off, Albert and his Olympia Academy friends talked while they ate a simple meal of sausage, cheese, fruit, honey, and tea. Sometimes they hiked or sat around in each other's apartments. Albert loved talking about his scientific ideas. It helped him to focus and refine his thoughts and to organize his ideas for publication. He used some of his

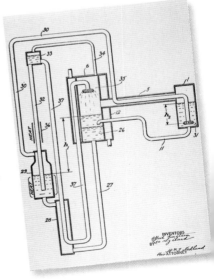

An inventor applying for a patent would submit a technical drawing of his invention.

ideas from his rejected Ph.D. dissertation and wrote a paper about the nature of the forces that keep molecules— tiny particles of matter too small to be seen by the eye— together in a liquid. He was pleased that it was published in September 1902 in the esteemed German physics journal, *Annalen der Physik*. Albert soon wrote two more scientific papers on the subject, and both were published. All his papers dealt with the new science of statistical mechanics. Albert wasn't aware that a scientist, William Gibbs, in the United States had published the same material.

The Importance of Being Published

In the early 1900s, just as in today's scientific community, having work published in respected journals or books was an important part of advancing an academic or scientific career. Albert Einstein was therefore hopeful and pleased that his ideas were published in prestigious scientific journals such as the *Annalen der Physik*. He knew that a steady record of publication would help him find future work in a university and gain acceptance in the scientific community.

Nevertheless, things were looking up for Albert. He had a job he enjoyed, good friends with whom to discuss ideas, and time to work on scientific papers for publication. Although Mileva was still in Hungary, they were in touch and he hoped they'd soon be reunited. But then, suddenly, Albert was summoned to Milan.

STATISTICAL MECHANICS

One of the subject areas of physics that combines the principles and procedures of statistics with the laws of mechanics.

The Einsteins enjoyed living in the picturesque old city of Bern, Switzerland. At one point they lived near the city's famous clocktower.

His father was gravely ill after a heart attack. Albert returned in time to see his father one final time. At their last meeting, his father gave Albert his blessing to marry Mileva. Shortly after, his father died. Hermann Einstein was only 55. Albert was devastated. He blamed the stress of business for his father's early death. He later referred to his father's death as the deepest shock he'd ever experienced.

Albert's father, who had never been very successful in business, had left his family in debt, and Pauline asked Albert to help her financially. She also felt forced to agree to Albert's marriage to Mileva.

Albert and Mileva were married on January 6, 1903, in Bern. Albert was 23 and Mileva was 27. Albert's mother and sister didn't attend the wedding. Albert's friends Maurice and Conrad were the only witnesses and guests. After the

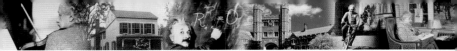

wedding, the four of them stayed out late celebrating. When Albert and Mileva finally returned to their new apartment on a quiet street, high

over the winding Aare River, Albert realized that he'd been absentminded again and had forgotten his keys. He had to ring the bell and awaken the tenants and landlord so they could enter the building.

Soon after his marriage, Albert wrote a fourth paper, this time on thermodynamics. He continued to meet with his friends for long talks that were often so noisy that the neighbors complained. Albert and his friends loved discussing science and philosophy through the night.

Albert and Mileva spent their honeymoon in Lausanne, Switzerland, an attractive city surrounded by forests, lakes, and mountains.

"Our means were frugal," Maurice recalled, "but our joy was boundless." Albert always felt that these meetings were an enriching part of his life and work.

In June 1903, Albert and Mileva decided to take a delayed honeymoon in Lausanne, Switzerland. While they were in Lausanne, Mileva discovered she was going to have another child. But this time Albert and Mileva had enough income to feel comfortable with the idea of being parents. They moved into a larger apartment with two rooms, near the famous clocktower in Bern. On May 14, 1904, Mileva gave birth to a boy they named Hans Albert.

Four months later, Albert heard that he would be promoted at the patent office. He would no longer be working on a trial basis but be placed on permanent staff, and his salary would be increased. He was pleased and

Albert and Mileva's first son, Hans Albert, was born in 1904.

relieved, especially since he now had a family to support.

Despite a new baby, a busy workload at the patent office, and meetings with friends, Albert still found time to work on his scientific ideas. He loved thinking about the answers to the questions about light, time, motion, and space that had consumed him since he was a boy. Nothing would stop him, certainly not the ordinary demands of domestic life. One visitor described the Einstein apartment as full of wet clothes strung across the kitchen and the smell of diapers, cigars, and smoke permeating the air. And yet the chaos didn't bother Albert. He could focus his attention on the scientific questions that interested him and forget his surroundings.

Amid the mess of his apartment, Albert always kept a space for studying and playing his violin.

chapter 7

A Miraculous Year

In 1905, Albert was 26, a husband, a father, and a civil servant working long hours. He had published a few papers, but he wasn't part of a university and he didn't work in a laboratory or have daily access to a major library. Instead, Albert worked alone grappling with questions he'd asked himself for years. What is light? Could a person travel as fast as light? What is time? Day after day, he looked at the established scientific theories and questioned them. Sometimes he was frustrated; at other times he was elated with the progress of his work.

But he never stopped looking for answers. In March, Albert sent a scientific paper to the *Annalen der Physik* journal. Most of the scientists of Albert's time believed that light traveled in waves. In his paper, Albert discussed experimental observations that the wave theory of light

Albert posed for this portrait in 1905, which was a busy year for him—in just twelve months, he published five important papers.

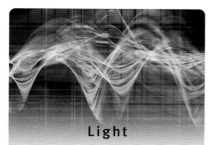

Light

Scientists have long debated about the nature of light. In the 17th century, English physicist Sir Isaac Newton said that light was formed by tiny particles traveling in a straight line. His theory was challenged by that of another scientist, Christian Huygens, who believed that light moved in waves through "ether," an invisible and weightless substance in the universe. Today, scientists believe that in different situations light can behave like either a particle or a wave. However, all scientists agree that the speed of light remains constant at 186,000 miles per second (300,000 km per second).

could not explain. The wave theory attributed the intensity and the energy of light to its brightness, not its color. But in an experiment, scientists found that blue light of high and low brightness produced an electric current between two metal plates, while red light of varying brightness did not. Albert explained this by theorizing that light acted as energized particles, termed "photons." The photons that made light blue or red differed in the energy they contained. Albert explained that the blue light's photons had sufficient energy to dislodge the electrons from the plate they struck and create an electric current when the dislodged electrons struck the second plate. The red light's photons did not have sufficient energy to produce an electric current. Albert's explanation is called the "photoelectric effect," and was a critical part of Albert's understanding of light as particles.

In April of the same year, Albert submitted a second paper called "A Determination of the Sizes of Molecules," which proved that molecules existed. He sent the second paper to Dr. Kleiner to be considered as a Ph.D. dissertation, but Dr. Kleiner rejected it for being too short.

In May, he submitted a third paper to the journal. This one was an explanation of Brownian motion, the phenomenon in which microscopic particles suspended in a fluid seem to move randomly. Robert Brown had observed this when small particles of pollen suspended in fluid seemed to jiggle or vibrate. Albert explained this phenomenon in terms of the impact that the surrounding fluid molecules had on the microscopic particles. He calculated the number of molecules involved and how fast they moved, then predicted how other liquids should behave. His predictions were shown to be correct two years later by the French physicist Jean Baptiste Perrin.

Albert was working feverishly. Ideas were coming to him so quickly, it was hard to find time to write them down.

Michele Besso was married to Anna Winteler, whom Einstein had known in Aarau. Einstein introduced the couple.

New ideas came to Albert so spontaneously that his papers were often messy and hard to read.

Sometimes when he was thinking, he became stumped and turned to pacing the floor or chewing on his cigar. Sometimes he was sure he'd never find the answer to a question and even told his friend Michele Besso that he was going to give up trying.

Michele, who had also begun working at the patent office, lived close by with his family. Albert and Michele spent hours talking. Michele, always a good sounding board, listened to Albert pursue his ideas and encouraged him not to give up.

One day that spring, Albert told Michele that he was close to figuring out a puzzle about distance and time. The next morning, Albert woke up excited. Albert's friend, Banesh Hoffman, describes how Albert reacted that wonderful day:

"Einstein said his basic discovery came on waking up one morning when he suddenly saw the idea. This had been going around and around at the back of his head for years and suddenly it wanted to thrust itself forward into his conscious mind."

Only one month later, in June, Albert wrote his fourth paper and submitted it to the *Annalen der Physik*. The paper, titled "The Special Theory of Relativity," argued that space and time are not absolute entities. Albert reasoned that the distance between two points and the elapsed time between two events are not the same for all observers throughout the universe. Instead, the speed of the observer, relative to the objects being measured, determines his or her perception of the distance between the objects. Similarly, the rate at which time seems to flow depends on how fast an observer is traveling—making the elapsed time between two events change from spectator to spectator. In other words, space and time are relative. Only one thing is a constant for all observers: the speed of light.

None of Einstein's papers were long, but they were all the foundations of new theories. He knew that many scientists might not agree with his ideas, but he was excited about them. Although he acknowledged his friend Michele's help in his papers, there were few references to anyone else.

He also knew his paper on special relativity was his most revolutionary and challenged basic scientific beliefs.

In September 1905, Albert's papers were published, and he waited anxiously for a reaction from the scientific community. At first, few scientists seemed to notice.

Albert wrote a fifth paper, stating that energy and mass were equivalent, which appeared in November 1905. Albert again waited for a reaction and again heard little. His sister Maja said: "Albert imagined that his publication in the renowned and much-read journals would draw immediate attention."

So far, it had not.

Einstein's theories followed in the footsteps of scientists such as Copernicus, whose controversial treatise (above) claimed that the Earth revolves around the sun.

chapter 8

Albert's Happiest Thought

In 1905, Albert revised his paper on the size of molecules by adding only one line and sent it to Professor Kleiner at the University of Zurich as his Ph.D. dissertation. This time, to Albert's amusement and delight, Professor Kleiner accepted his work, and Albert officially became Dr. Einstein. In April 1906, he was promoted to technical expert second class at the patent office, and his new promotion came with a higher salary. Life at home was better, too. He helped Mileva with household chores, splitting wood, carrying it up to the oven, and playing with mischievous two-year-old Hans Albert.

Despite the new responsibilities that came with his promotion, Albert still had time to work on his own scientific ideas. He even kept a

In 1946, years after Albert first published his famous formula $E=mc^2$, he wrote this article discussing the dangers of using matter to create nuclear energy.

drawer in his desk at the patent office for his sketches and equations, which he called his "Department of Physics." Albert probably didn't tell Director Haller that he was jotting down notes on his physics ideas while attending to his office duties. Somehow he managed to do both successfully.

Max Planck

Max Planck (1858–1947) was a great German physicist who received the Nobel Prize in Physics in 1918 for showing the connection between energy and temperature. Einstein's work on the quantum theory builds on Planck's work.

Albert was also pleased that famous scientists such as Max Planck were taking notice of his work on relativity. Maybe now with a Ph.D., scientific papers published in prestigious journals, and the attention of respected scientists, he could get a teaching job as a privatdozent at the University of Bern. Although being a privatdozent was only a part-time position in which lecturers were paid a small amount directly by students, it was an important stepping-stone to other teaching jobs. But when Albert applied, the university turned him down. The department head, Aime Foster, felt that Albert's relativity paper was "incomprehensible."

Albert didn't let that disappointment bother him. He was

$$E = mc^2$$

Einstein's equation relating mass and energy may be the most famous equation ever written. It explains how much energy a given object can produce. Even an object with a very small mass can generate a great deal of energy when multiplied by a number as large as the speed of light. Scientists have used this equation to develop atomic energy, figure out why the stars shine, and create the atom bomb, the most destructive weapon ever made.

too busy working on new ideas. After pondering an idea for more than two years, he now formulated an equation, $E=mc^2$, which stated that mass (m) and energy (E) are equivalent, but that they differ in form. This means that one can be converted into the other. To calculate the energy, the object's mass must be multiplied by c^2, which is the speed of light (186,000 miles per second or 300,000 kilometers per second) multiplied by itself—a huge amount. Albert included this equation in an article for the *Annalen der Physik*.

Then, in 1907, Albert had what he called his "happiest thought," an idea that started him thinking about gravity. Albert describes his breakthrough: "I was sitting on a chair in my patent office in Bern. Suddenly, a thought struck me: If a man falls freely he would not feel his weight. I was taken aback." Albert again used a "thought experiment" to solve an intriguing problem. He understood that a man falling freely through air would feel weightless as he accelerated toward the ground. This led him to conclude that gravity (the force of the earth's pull on all objects) and acceleration (the force of an object falling freely) are equivalent. He called this the "Equivalence Principle."

That year, with increased scientific interest in his theories, Albert decided to apply to become a privatdozent again. This time, the University of Bern hired him. Since it was only a part-time position, he still had to work at the patent office. He also had to schedule classes for odd hours, like seven or eight o'clock in the morning. Not too many people wanted to attend classes that early, so Albert had few students. The next year, he gave one course where the only people who turned up were his friend Michele Besso and his sister, Maja.

By 1908, Albert's work was becoming discussed widely in the northern European scientific community. When scientists gathered at the 80th Congress of Natural Scientists in Cologne, Germany, although Albert wasn't present, his theory of relativity created a lot of interest. Even Albert's former mathematics professor, Hermann Minkowski, was excited by Albert's theory. He was also astounded that his "lazy dog" of a student had formulated it. "Oh that Einstein," he said, "always cutting lectures. I really would not have believed him capable of it."

Despite his rumpled appearance, Albert became one of the University of Zurich's most popular professors.

That same year, Albert and his friend Conrad Habicht tinkered with an electric device to make it measure tiny electric charges. If it worked, they were certain that laboratories would be clamoring to use it. Albert called it the *maschinchen* ("little machine") and Albert and Conrad took out a patent. Conrad manufactured and sold versions of the *maschinchen* for many years, but it never worked smoothly enough to be a real success.

Meanwhile, Albert's fame was growing, and he was offered a full-time teaching position at the prestigious University of Zurich. He almost didn't get the job. His Ph.D. adviser, Professor Kleiner, came to see him teach in Bern on behalf of the university. The day he arrived, Albert had only one student.

The University of Zurich was the first European university founded by a democratic state instead of a church or monarch. When Einstein attended, it had about one thousand students.

Albert was dressed in a scruffy outfit and was unprepared

for the lecture. He was also nervous knowing that he was being observed. Professor Kleiner reported back to the university that Albert was an unsatisfactory teacher, and Albert had to ask him to reconsider his evaluation. Albert was given another chance to show his teaching skill. This time he spoke in front of the Zurich Physical Society and performed well. He said: "I was lucky; contrary to my habit, I lectured well on this occasion."

Albert's salary at the University of Zurich was the same as he had earned at the patent office, but it didn't matter. It was time for a change. After all, Albert didn't want to remain a patent clerk all his life. In 1909, he resigned from the patent office and, at the age of 30, became an associate professor.

Although Albert was now teaching at a major university, he still dressed in baggy old pants that were often too short for his legs, and he wrote his lecture notes on scraps of paper. At first some of the students commented on his strange outfits and habits, but they soon grew to respect his good humor, friendly manner, and open approach to teaching. He was always ready to answer questions and often socialized with students at cafés or at his new apartment on Moussonstrasse. After classes he'd often say: "Who's coming to the Café Terrasse?" Once Albert and his students stayed till the café closed for the night. One of his students, Hans Tanner, said that, despite his informal appearance, "After the first few sentences he captured our hearts."

Not all of Albert's fellow professors approved of his casual style, but Albert enjoyed teaching this way. After many years of being uncomfortable in a school setting, he was finally at ease.

In 1909, Albert was nominated for the Nobel Prize by Nobel laureate Wilhelm Ostwald. Ostwald had previously rejected Albert's application to be his assistant in 1901. Now Ostwald told the Nobel Committee that Einstein's Special Theory of Relativity was a major scientific contribution. Although Albert didn't win the Nobel that year, it was clear that his life and standing in the scientific community had

Prague's grand buildings were beautiful, but as foreigners, Albert and Mileva found the city cold and unwelcoming.

changed in the eight years since Ostwald turned him down.

On July 28, 1910, Mileva gave birth to the Einsteins' second son, whom they named Eduard. Albert's life was busy and full. He had a wife, children, friends, his work at the university, and his own scientific studies. To relax, he played the violin and sailed around the beautiful Zurich lakes. In 1910, he also wrote another paper that dealt with the question so many children ask: Why is the sky blue? Albert's explanation was simple. Air molecules scatter blue sunlight more than any other color. This blue sunlight appears to be coming to us from all directions, and that's why the sky is blue. Once again, Albert's theory was rooted in questioning everyday phenomena.

Albert didn't stay in Zurich long. He was soon asked to become a full professor at the German University in Prague. Mileva didn't want to move to Prague. She was happy in

Zurich. Both she and Albert felt they would be foreigners in Prague, a city divided between its Czech and German populations. They knew that the two groups rarely mixed, and the Jewish population, caught between the Czechs and Germans, was not welcomed by either group. Despite their reservations, Albert accepted the position.

Franz Kafka

Franz Kafka (1883–1924), who lived in Prague, was one of the most influential writers in the German language. He was trained as a lawyer and worked for an insurance company, but he wrote whenever he could. Much of his work was published after his death in 1924 from tuberculosis. Kafka wrote in a surrealistic, symbolic style.

Albert and Mileva found Prague as unwelcoming as they had anticipated, but Albert had an influential position with a higher salary and excellent research facilities at his disposal. He wrote to his friend Michele Besso: "My position and my institute give me much joy, only the people are so alien to me." Albert made many friends within Prague's Jewish intellectual community, often with people who didn't have anything to do with science. One of his friends was the writer Franz Kafka,

Mileva stayed home to take care of the Einsteins' two young sons, Eduard and Hans Albert.

who, like Albert, had produced brilliant work while earning his living at a mundane job.

Albert met with renowned scientists at the Solvay conference in Brussels in 1911.

Soon Albert was attending scientific conferences outside Prague, leaving Mileva at home with the boys. Mileva felt alone and lonely. She wrote to Albert: "I would have loved only too much to have listened a little and to have seen all those fine people. It has been an eternity since we have seen each other. Will you still recognize me?"

In 1911, Albert attended the Solvay conference in Brussels, where he spoke to such famous physicists as Marie Curie, Ernest Rutherford, and Max Planck. At the age of 32, Albert was one of the youngest scientists attending the conference. After only a few years, he'd gone from being an unknown clerk with few scientific credentials to one of the most sought-after scientists of his time.

chapter 9

New Opportunities, New Dilemmas

In 1911, Albert's old classmate Marcel Grossmann, now the dean of physics at the Swiss Polytechnic, offered Albert a teaching position. Albert and Mileva were delighted to accept the job and return to Zurich. Albert was especially pleased at the chance to return as a success to a school where he had had difficulties as a student. It felt wonderful to be welcomed as a respected professor.

Although Albert and Mileva were happy to live in Zurich again and had a spacious apartment with many comforts, they were unhappy living together. Mileva never passed her Polytechnic exams, so she never received her degree. Instead, she stayed at home with two demanding children while Albert was increasingly involved in teaching and science.

Albert spent three semesters teaching in Zurich, but much of his time and energy were devoted to working on his theory of gravitation. He was also nominated for the Nobel Prize in Physics for the second time, but despite upport in the scientific community, he didn't receive the award. However, his reputation was growing, and he was soon offered a professorship in Berlin. It was a job that would allow Albert to spend time working on his scientific ideas

Marie Curie

Marie Curie (1867–1934) was born in Poland and later worked in Paris with her husband, Pierre Curie. Together they discovered radium, for which they jointly won the Nobel Prize in 1903 (the first ever awarded to a woman). In 1911, Marie Curie won a second Nobel Prize in Chemistry. She died from a blood cancer, probably caused by direct contact with radium.

with only a few teaching responsibilities, and it came with an even higher salary.

Before Albert agreed to take the job, Albert, Mileva, and Hans Albert spent a summer holiday hiking with their friend Marie Curie. While they were walking up hills or through the woods, Albert was often so absorbed in conversation or his thoughts that he barely noticed the steep path or boulders in his way. Once he stopped suddenly and turned to Marie Curie. "You understand," he said, "what I need to know is exactly what happens to an elevator when it falls into emptiness."

In December 1913, Albert formally agreed to take the professorship in Berlin. Mileva wasn't happy about the move. It meant she would be in the same city as Albert's mother, who, despite all the time that had passed, still disapproved of Mileva. Albert said: "My wife howls unceasingly about Berlin and her fear of my relatives....Well, there is some truth in it.

My mother is of a good disposition on the whole but a true devil as a mother-in-law."

Not long after Albert agreed to the job offer, the Einsteins moved. But Mileva felt neglected and depressed, and decided to return to Zurich with the boys just as World War I was about to erupt. Soon travel between warring Germany and neutral Switzerland became increasingly difficult and made it hard for Albert to visit his children. Albert, who'd always opposed war and militaristic policies, was one of only a few scientists in Germany to express anti-war sentiments.

Albert missed his sons and wrote letters encouraging them to take care of themselves and to work hard at their studies. However, despite the separation from his family and the war engulfing Europe, Albert enjoyed the quiet and calm of his bachelor apartment in Berlin. He continued to work long hours on his theories and was often so absorbed in his work that he skipped meals. When he did cook, his meal was often a hodgepodge of ingredients hastily dumped into one

In the summer of 1924, Albert met with Robert Millikan and Marie Curie to exchange new scientific ideas.

big pot. He was also
developing a friendship
with his divorced cousin,
Elsa, who lived in Berlin
with her two daughters.

As the war raged
on, Albert's family life
deteriorated. Albert
wanted a divorce, but
Mileva still hoped they
would reconcile. His sons
refused to correspond with
him and continued to be a
source of worry—especially
Eduard, who was a sickly
and shy child.

Despite everything,
during the 15 months from
November 1915 to February
1917, Albert produced 15
scientific papers—among
them, the General Theory of
Relativity on which he had been working for so long. In his
General Theory of Relativity, Albert returned to examining
the concepts of time and space that he first explored in his
Special Theory of Relativity in 1905. The Special Theory of
Relativity had indicated that the measurement of space and

World War I

Sparked by the assassination of
Archduke Ferdinand of Austria-
Hungary by a Serbian terrorist,
the conflict that became known
as "the Great War" grew to
involve more countries than any
war before it—and take nine
million lives. The Central
powers, led by Germany and
Austria-Hungary, fought the
Allied forces, led by France,
Russia, and Britain. The United
States joined the Allied forces in
1917, when President Wilson
called on Americans to "make
the world safe for democracy."

time were not absolutes, but were relative to the motion of observers. What was constant was the speed of light. But the Special Theory was based on the assumption that observers and objects were moving uniformly, that is at a constant speed relative to one another. In his General Theory, Albert turned from the special case of uniform motion to the general effect of acceleration. He still argued that motion affected the measurement of time and space. In the General Theory, he also added that the effect of gravity is equal to the effect of acceleration, and so gravity, too, affected the measurement of time and space. According to Albert's theory, the gravitational effect of the sun would bend the path of starlight.

In 1916, Albert was again nominated for the Nobel Prize, but because of the ongoing war, the judges decided not to award the prize to anyone.

Hard work and personal problems finally took their toll on Albert's health. In 1917, he collapsed and was diagnosed with gallstones. His cousin Elsa took care of him as he

Albert Einstein strikes a pose in his study in Berlin in 1916.

spent months recovering. But even during his illness, Albert continued to work.

In 1918, the war ended, and Albert and Mileva were finally divorced. In the divorce settlement, Albert promised Mileva any future proceeds from the Nobel Prize. By now, he'd been nominated so many times, he thought there was a good chance he would eventually win.

Soon after his divorce, Albert married Elsa. She set about fixing up their apartment. There was one room, though, that she was

Albert's second wife, Elsa Einstein Loewenthal, worked hard to shield Albert from the pressures of fame.

not allowed to touch: Albert's study was full of his papers, books, and journals. A desk and chair were placed near the window, and prints of famous scientists hung on the wall. It was Albert's private retreat.

As always, Albert continued to be absentminded. Once, when Albert stayed in the bathroom for more than an hour, his stepdaughter Margot worried that he had fallen. But Albert was fine; he'd just been so wrapped up in his thoughts that he'd forgotten he was still soaking in the tub.

chapter 10

Fame

By 1919, Albert was well known within the scientific community and in Germany, but not in other parts of the world. Arthur Eddington and his 1919 expedition would change all that.

Eddington, a famous English astronomer, and Sir Frances Dyson, the Astronomer Royal of England, felt that during an eclipse of the sun it would be possible to test the most dramatic aspect of Albert's General Theory of Relativity: the idea that a beam of light passing near the sun bends because of the pull of the sun's gravity. A solar eclipse was expected to occur in May 1919. That month, Eddington led an expedition to Principe, a small island off western

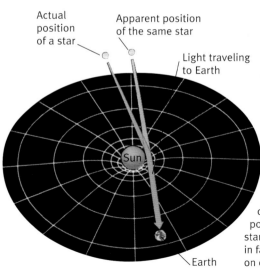

Actual position of a star

Apparent position of the same star

Light traveling to Earth

Sun

Earth

This diagram shows how the gravitational pull of the sun causes the light from a star to follow a curved path, making its apparent position different from its actual position. This curve allows the star to be visible from Earth, when in fact the star and the Earth are on opposite sides of the sun.

Solar Eclipse

A solar eclipse occurs when the earth, moon, and sun are aligned in a special way. In this arrangement, the moon is between the earth and the sun so that the face of the moon is darkened and the sun appears as a bright disc behind the moon.

Africa, while a colleague led a second expedition to Sobral, Brazil. The two teams would take photographs of the eclipse to measure the behavior of light in relation to the sun and stars. By comparing photographs taken during the eclipse with each other, and then comparing both sets with photographs taken six months earlier, it would be possible to determine if the path of a beam of light was bent as it passed close to the edge of the sun.

On the day of the eclipse it was raining and cloudy, making it difficult to take the necessary photographs in Principe. Eddington waited anxiously for a break in the clouds. When it came, he quickly took pictures. Only one photograph appeared to confirm Albert's theory. Eddington sent a telegraph to his colleagues in London: "Through clouds hopeful. Eddington." Eddington's

Arthur Eddington was a leading astrophysicist of his day. He was one of the first scientists to understand Einstein's early theories. In 1930, he would become Sir Arthur Eddington.

Sir Isaac Newton

Isaac Newton was one of the foremost mathematicians and physicists of all time. He defined three basic laws of gravity and motion, which he used to predict the motion of the stars and planets around the sun. Newton's laws were widely adopted by physicists in his day, and are still important to scientific study today. Newton was buried in Westminster Abbey in London, England. He was the first scientist to be given such an honor.

measurements would have to be confirmed in England before an announcement could be made. He hoped the results of the Sobral expedition would be even more conclusive. To his delight, seven of the Sobral photographs seemed to confirm Albert's predictions. It was now up to the Royal Society and Royal Astronomical Society to make the final judgment.

The two organizations met on November 6, 1919, in a London hall packed with scientists and reporters. Dyson began speaking: "After careful study of the photos, I am prepared to say that there can be no doubt that they confirm Einstein's predictions." The president of the Royal Society, J. J. Thomson, said, "This is one of the most important results obtained in connection with the theory of gravitation since Newton's day. It is one of the highest achievements of human thought."

Eddington wrote a verse celebrating the event:

One thing at least is certain. Light has weight.
One thing is certain and the rest debate-
Light rays, when near the sun, DO NOT GO STRAIGHT.

On November 7, the *Times of London* headline announced a "Revolution in Science—New Theory of the Universe—Newton's Ideas Overthrown." Soon the *New York Times* picked up the story, followed by hundreds of newspapers around the world.

Overnight, Albert became a world celebrity, catapulting from private citizen to public figure. But at the same time that many hailed Albert's theories as brilliant and revolutionary, others questioned their accuracy. Some even suggested that they were closer to science fiction than reality, and thought that perhaps Albert had borrowed his concepts from popular fantasy books.

Albert refused to become involved in the controversies. He realized that fame can be fleeting, and that people perceive individuals and ideas through their own expectations and experiences. "At present every coachman and every waiter argues whether or not the relativity theory is correct," he noted. "A person's conviction on this point depends on the political party he belongs."

Einstein tried to take his celebrity in stride, realizing that the public would sway to whatever opinions were popular.

The Weimar Republic was the first attempt at establishing a liberal democracy in Germany. It lasted from 1911 until 1933 during a time of economic and political turmoil. The rise of the Nazi party in 1933 put an end to the Weimar Republic.

While all this public interest was going on, Albert's mother, Pauline, was dying of cancer and spending her final days with Albert and Elsa. Mileva, who still lived in Switzerland, continued to have financial problems, and Eduard, who had always been a sickly child, was recuperating in a hospital for people with serious illnesses. Eduard had a remarkable memory and a bright mind, but his constant earaches and severe mood swings required expensive hospitalizations. Albert's finances were stretched to the limit trying to provide for his scattered family.

Albert was also concerned about the political atmosphere in Germany after its defeat in World War I. He supported the new government, the Weimar Republic, but was discomforted by rumors in the press and on the street that the Weimar Republic and the Jews were responsible for the difficult conditions in Germany. "There is strong anti-Semitism here," he wrote. Albert felt that the peace treaty the Allied powers had imposed on Germany was overly harsh and was helping create a chaotic atmosphere. Germany had rampant inflation, high unemployment, and, worst of all, the Nazis, members of a new racist political party, were gaining influence and power.

Albert, who was now one of the most famous Germans in the world, found that public opponents of his theories were often also his political opponents. He tried not to overreact to the accusations that he was a publicity hound and that his theories were rubbish or science fiction. He tried to keep working, but it was hard amid the constant media attention. "Scientifically, I don't have much to show at the moment," he wrote. "My life is too hectic."

During this time, Albert became involved with Zionism, a movement to establish a Jewish national state in Palestine (now called Israel). Albert met the Zionist leader Chaim Weizmann in Berlin. In 1917, Weizmann had persuaded the British government to help make Palestine a homeland for the Jews, and he now asked Albert and Elsa to join him on a trip to the United States to help him raise money for a new university in Jerusalem.

At first Albert was reluctant. He didn't feel comfortable fundraising. But eventually he became convinced that a Jewish homeland would help Jews around the world find a safe refuge from discrimination, and he agreed. He and Elsa would go to America.

Zionist leader Chaim Weizmann and Albert Einstein arrive in America.

11

Einstein Fever

Albert, Elsa, Chaim Weizmann, and Weizmann's wife, Vera, sailed to New York aboard the *Rotterdam* in April 1921. When they landed, reporters converged on the ship, bombarding Albert with questions that he had difficulty answering in English. They also asked Dr. Weizmann if he understood Albert's theories. Weizmann, who was a distinguished chemist, jokingly replied: "During our crossing, Einstein explained his theory to me every day, and on our arrival, I realized that he really understood it."

Crowds surrounded the Einsteins wherever they went. The press and public enjoyed Albert's good-natured and patient responses to their endless questions. Despite the crowds and the demands of the media, Albert enjoyed New York. He liked the bright lights, the billboards, the many different ethnic restaurants, and the healthy-looking people. It was a wonderful contrast

Einstein received a warm reception when he arrived in New York in 1921.

An audience member wrote down this summary of one of Einstein's lectures: "There is no hitching post in the Universe—so far as we know." The paper is signed by Einstein.

to drab, war-ravaged Berlin. He was also delighted that one of the people who came to see him was his old mentor and friend, the man who had introduced him to science books and geometry, Max Talmud. Max, who now called himself Max Talmey, was a successful physician living in New York.

Thousands of people squeezed into the 69th Regiment Armory in Manhattan on April 12 to hear Albert and Weizmann speak, and more people waited outside to catch a glimpse of the famous scientist. Then Albert and Weizmann traveled to other American cities, lecturing and raising funds. On his trip, Albert spoke with American scientists in Chicago, Illinois; Washington, D.C.; and Princeton, New Jersey. Everywhere he traveled, he was bombarded with questions and requests for interviews. He continued to show great patience, humor, and grace. Once Albert was asked by a reporter, "What is the speed of sound?" and he answered: "I don't know offhand. I don't carry information in my mind that's readily available in books."

This view differed dramatically from that of famous inventor Thomas Edison, who at the time was touting the

Thomas Edison

Thomas Edison was an American inventor and businessman who patented 1,093 inventions in his name. His most famous invention was the lightbulb. Edison believed in hard work and said, "Genius is one percent inspiration and 99 percent perspiration."

importance of acquiring facts and remembering information as the key to success. Edison was so convinced of his opinion that he insisted that those seeking work with him had to first answer 150 questions. Einstein disagreed. He believed that the value of a good education is that it trains the mind to think.

After spending more than a month in the United States, the Einsteins sailed to England. There Albert met famous scientists, politicians, actors, writers, and even church dignitaries.

When Albert returned home, he vacationed with his two sons, 17-year-old Hans Albert and 11-year-old Eduard. He was glad that his relationships with Mileva and his boys were finally more relaxed.

Albert's next stop was Paris. He received a mixed reception. The French press was generally enthusiastic and welcoming, but there were also threats made against him. Albert was finding once again that reaction to him was often less about his scientific views and more about his political views and his Jewish background.

While Albert was traveling around Europe, his friend Walter Rathenau, the German minister of foreign affairs, received death threats from those who believed that Germany could and should stand alone in the world. Rathenau disregarded the danger and continued to speak out publicly about his belief in international cooperation. In April 1922, Rathenau signed a treaty

Albert spoke at the Royal Albert Hall in London, England. He enjoyed meeting scientists, politicians, and other dignitaries as he traveled through Europe.

establishing renewed German diplomatic relations with Russia and promising economic cooperation. With that act, the death threats increased. Some people accused Rathenau of selling out the German people to the Russian Communist government.

On June 24, 1922, Rathenau was gunned down. Rumors flew that Albert, who shared many of Rathenau's political beliefs and high profile, might be the next target.

Walter Rathenau worked to fulfill Germany's World War I reparations requirements, making him unpopular with many German nationalists.

12

Nobel Prize

For a number of years, Albert had believed that there had to be a common thread that linked all physical forces. Early in 1922, he wrote a short paper on the subject outlining his "unified field theory" for a force he had yet to define. The quest for a unified theory would absorb him for the rest of his life.

On November 9, 1922, while traveling between Hong Kong and Shanghai on the lecture circuit, Albert learned that he'd won the Nobel Prize in Physics. Despite having been nominated so many times before, he was sincerely delighted that he'd finally won.

Why had it taken so long for Albert to win the Nobel Prize? Some people thought that Nobel laureate Philipp Lenard's anti-Semitism had prejudiced the committee. Others noted the rules laid down by Alfred Nobel, which required that the prize be given to a scientist whose discovery benefited humankind in a direct way. The Nobel committee could not see the practical application of relativity— in fact, some were unclear about its very meaning. In the end, Albert didn't

Scientists flocked to hear Albert Einstein lecture about his theories.

receive the prize for his famous relativity theory. Instead, the committee cited "his services to theoretical physics and especially for his discovery of the law of the photoelectric effect." Since Albert was in the middle of his Far Eastern tour, he couldn't personally accept the award. But as promised, he gave Mileva all the prize money.

The Nobel Prize medal bears Alfred Nobel's likeness.

As Albert continued his tour, he stopped in Palestine, where he spoke at the site of the future Hebrew University. He traveled around the small country marveling at how an arid land was being transformed by hard work into a livable country and noted, "the difficulties are great but the mood is confident and the work to be marveled at."

After leaving Palestine, Albert visited Spain, where he was greeted with great enthusiasm. The entire trip seemed like an amazing dream to him. "Let's enjoy everything before we wake up," he told Elsa.

As Albert continued to travel through Europe, events in Germany were taking a dramatic turn. Nazi leader Adolf Hitler made an attempt to take over the German government. Although his attempt was unsuccessful and Hitler was jailed for

Albert traveled to Palestine and spoke in Jerusalem on Mount Scopus, the site of the future Hebrew University.

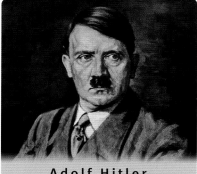

Adolf Hitler

Adolf Hitler (1889–1945) was the leader of the Nazi party in Germany and head of the German government from 1933 to 1945. He ruled as a dictator and invaded neighboring countries in Europe such as Czechoslovakia and Poland, starting World War II. He also ordered the murder of millions of innocent people, including six million Jews in the Holocaust.

treason, it was clear that the seeds of political change were sprouting in Germany.

In May 1925, Albert and Elsa sailed to South America, and Albert lectured to college audiences in Buenos Aires, Rio de Janeiro, and Montevideo. While traveling, Albert wrote letters to his sons. He worried about Hans Albert, who had no job prospects and was determined to marry a woman nine years his senior. He was concerned about Eduard, who had a remarkable memory and intellect but often behaved strangely.

Albert was fearful that Eduard had inherited the mental problems that plagued Mileva's sister, Zorka.

Over the next few years, Albert worked on his scientific ideas while lecturing and meeting other thinkers and scientists. He became friends with Sigmund Freud, the man who introduced psychoanalytic theory to the world, and Niels Bohr, a Danish physicist who won the Nobel Prize a

PACIFIST

A pacifist is a person opposed to war or violence as a means of settling disputes between countries.

year after Albert. He also continued to speak out for peace and to believe that nothing could justify using arms against people.

In 1928, while on a trip to Davos, Switzerland, Albert collapsed. He was diagnosed with a heart condition, and the doctors told him to relax. When he returned to Berlin, Elsa found she couldn't cope with the demands of running a household, answering Albert's massive correspondence, and caring for Albert while he recovered, so Albert hired a secretary, Helen Dukas. At first, Helen was nervous about meeting and working with such an esteemed scientist, but Albert's charm and easygoing manner soon put her at ease. She was also greatly relieved that a knowledge of science was not a requirement for the job.

In 1929, as Albert recovered, the world was hit by a severe economic depression. Germany suffered further economic hardship, and attacks against Jews increased. Albert tried to help people whose lives were affected by anti-Semitism.

Helen Dukas began working for Albert when he was 50 years old. She would work for him for the rest of his life.

chapter 13

Nazi Party

In 1929, Albert turned 50, and the Berlin authorities offered to give him a gift of land to acknowledge his scientific contributions. Albert loved sailing, so they chose a plot of land on the river Havel, near the village of Caputh. Albert and Elsa spent their own funds to build a house there. They loved the beauty and tranquillity of the area and their comfortable new home. They enjoyed many happy days there.

In 1931, Albert traveled to California as a visiting professor at the California Institute of Technology, where he met scientists such as Edwin Hubble, who was working with a powerful telescope to study the galaxies and the expansion of the universe. Albert's General Theory of Relativity had predicted the expansion before Hubble found it. Albert at first refused to believe his own theory,

Albert and Elsa loved their country home in Caputh, and spent many happy hours sailing, reading, walking, and welcoming visitors.

tinkering with General Relativity to make the expansion aspect disappear. He later called that effort the biggest mistake of his life.

After two months of "loafing in Paradise," as Albert said, the Einsteins headed for New York. The pair stopped at the Grand Canyon on the way, and Albert was initiated into a Hopi Indian tribe as a chief named "The Great Relative" and tried on a full Indian headdress for the occasion.

After his travels abroad, Albert would always return to his idyllic country retreat at Caputh in an attempt to escape the increasingly ugly and threatening atmosphere in Germany. Despite the political unrest, Albert never stopped speaking out on issues like civil rights and disarmament, a policy of giving up weapons as a means to promote peace. He intervened where he felt injustice had been done to individuals—not just in Europe, but in the United States as well. He spoke up in the Scottsboro, Alabama, case against eight black youths who faced execution for allegedly raping two white girls, despite flimsy evidence.

By 1931, Adolf Hitler and the Nazi Party were becoming more powerful in Germany. Hitler's message of renewing Germany's past glory and the supremacy of the German people appealed to many who were still faced with deep financial difficulties, huge unemployment, and chaos since World War I. As Albert watched the Nazis gain power and as he read the pro-Hitler newspapers, he became convinced that he would have to leave Germany. He loved Caputh, but he sensed that, as a Jew, it would be too dangerous to stay.

Albert was approached by an American scientific administrator, Abraham Flexner, who was eager to set up an institute for advanced research in Princeton, New Jersey. Flexner wanted to establish a place where great scientists could work undisturbed to pursue their scientific ideas. Despite the political situation in Germany, at first Albert wasn't ready to accept Flexner's proposal.

That summer in Caputh, the Einsteins' visitors included Thomas Bucky, the 13-year-old son of a family friend. Albert treated Thomas with great warmth, and the young boy felt that Albert was almost like a second father to him. Thomas later described his happy visit with the Einsteins: "I didn't hesitate to discuss politics with him and express my opinions, and was never afraid to challenge him in debate for he welcomed even the perhaps half-baked opinion of a teenager. He was very tolerant, but he despised yes-men....And he hated dictatorships of the right or left."

Thomas also described Albert's personality. "I never saw him lose his temper, never saw him angry or bitter, or vain or jealous, worried, impatient or personally ambitious. He seemed immune to such feelings. But he had a shy attitude toward everybody....Einstein had a shell around him that was not easy to penetrate." One person Albert was especially close to was his sister, Maja. Bucky noted how much alike the two were: "They looked alike, with the same mane of hair, and laughed and talked alike. She was extremely intelligent and more accessible than her genius brother...."

In the summer of 1932, Nazi students protested the presence of Jewish students and teachers in German universities. Albert's friends, including Flexner, encouraged him to leave Germany, but he still wasn't ready. Elsa begged Albert to stop signing anti-war petitions and to be more cautious about his anti-Nazi views, but Albert refused. However, as the Nazis became the strongest power in Germany, Albert began to reconsider his decision about the job offer in Princeton. He told Flexner that he would accept the job if his scientific associate and assistant,

Like her brother, Maja Einstein pursued an advanced academic degree. She received her PhD in romance languages from the University of Bern.

Walter Mayer, could join him in Princeton.

By December 1932, the elderly president of Germany, Paul von Hindenburg, was being pushed out of office by the Nazis, and Nazi storm troopers, members of a private Nazi army notorious for brutality, were roughing people up in the streets. That month, Albert and Elsa finally left Caputh. As he left the house, Albert turned to Elsa and said, "Before you leave our villa this time, take a good look at it. You will never see it again." He knew that the Nazis were about to gain total power in Germany, and that returning there would be impossible.

In January 1933, President Hindenburg was persuaded by a coalition of Nazis and right-wing politicians to appoint Hitler as chancellor of Germany. By March, the Weimar Republic was dead, and the Third Reich, a Fascist political state, rose in its place. In only a few months, Hitler abolished all civil liberties, destroyed rival political rivals, and built concentration camps. The Gestapo, Hitler's secret police, used force to quell any opposition.

Albert was visiting Albany, New York, when he heard that Nazi storm troopers had ransacked his Berlin apartment five times in two days, terrifying his stepdaughters, Ilse and Margot. The Gestapo looked for documents they could use against him, but Ilse and Margot had smuggled his most important papers to the French embassy in Berlin. Storm troopers also searched his country house in Caputh and again found nothing.

Despite these events and vicious articles in the German press about him, Albert kept speaking out against war and the militaristic Nazi regime. In March 1933, Albert resigned from the Prussian Academy of Science just before they expelled him, and, in April, he resigned from the Bavarian

Academy of Science. He said in a public statement: "As long as I have any choice in the matter, I shall live in a country where civil liberty, tolerance, and equality of all citizens before the law prevail....These conditions do not exist in Germany at the present time."

Nazi outrages continued. On April 1, 1933, Einstein's property was seized and a reward offered for his capture as an enemy of the state. The Nobel laureate Phillipp Lenard, who had long hated and opposed Albert, denounced him and all Jews and their theories.

Concentration Camps

A concentration camp is a large center used to detain people because of ethnic, political, or religious beliefs or origins. During World War II, the Nazi regime set up concentration camps where prisoners were killed in gas chambers, shot, or worked to death. It is estimated that more than 10 million people were killed by the Nazis in these camps.

Soon after, the Nazis beat up customers entering Jewish-owned shops, and in May tens of thousands of Germans poured into a public square in Berlin and burned books in a giant bonfire. The books were written not only by Jewish writers and thinkers like Einstein, but by major international authors such as Jack London, Helen Keller, H. G. Wells, Ernest Hemingway, and Upton Sinclair. The Nazis hoped to further stifle the free flow of ideas and opinions, especially those that were in direct conflict with Nazi beliefs.

Albert was concerned about his family and encouraged Ilse and Margot to leave Germany for France. But it wasn't only the political situation that made him worry about his family. His son, Eduard, who still lived in Zurich, was sliding into schizophrenia, a severe mental illness.

In 1933 the Nazi regime in Germany instigated a mass burning of books by Jewish and non-Jewish writers.

After his trip to the United States, Albert visited England and met with Winston Churchill, an influential conservative member of Parliament. Albert warned Churchill that Hitler was preparing to go to war. He felt confident that Churchill had similar concerns and would help act on them. Soon many of Albert's former assistants and colleagues in

Albert visited conservative member of English parliament Winston Churchill, who shared his concerns about Germany and the Nazi Party.

Germany were tossed out of their positions. Many left Germany for the United States or England.

Meanwhile, Albert visited Belgium, renewing his long-standing friendship with Queen Elizabeth of Belgium. The Belgian Royal family provided protection for Albert and Elsa, but events were moving quickly in Europe. Albert knew there would be war, and he knew how dangerous the Nazis were to all of Europe and the world. He also realized that he had to reexamine his pacifist views. He now

Winston Churchill

Winston Churchill was an important British politician, writer and speaker. As prime minister, he led Britain during World War II and had a strong relationship with President Franklin Roosevelt of the United States. Britain and the United States worked together to defeat the Nazis and Fascists. Churchill also received the 1953 Nobel Prize for Literature.

believed that there were some enemies that had to be militarily defeated, and the Nazis were such an enemy. He told Belgian pacifists: "If I were Belgian, I'd not refuse military service under the present circumstances. Today Germany is preparing for war by every means." Albert now believed that every citizen needed to accept military service to combat a regime that wanted to destroy European civilization and freedom.

chapter **14**

The March to War

In the late spring of 1933, the Nazi regime printed a list of enemies of the state with Albert's name at the top. Under his photograph were the words "not yet hanged."

In October 1933, Albert gave a talk in London to a packed auditorium of 10,000 in the Royal Albert Hall. The hall was heavily guarded, because rumors circulated that there would be an attempt on Albert's life. Albert spoke passionately in support of the Academic Alliance Council, a group that assisted refugee students who could not continue their education because of the political climate. In his speech he repeated his long-held belief in education and the right of individuals to study in a free society. He thanked the British for remaining loyal to their tradition of justice and tolerance. He hoped that people in the future would note "that in our day the freedom and honor of this continent was saved by its western nations." Soon

While in England, Albert stayed at the holiday camp of Commander Oliver L. Lampson, who hired armed guards to protect Albert from Nazi threats.

after, Albert and Elsa sailed to the United States. Albert would never return to Europe.

Professors Eisenhart and Mayer worked with Albert at Princeton, where he took a position at the Institute for Advanced Study.

Although many Americans welcomed Albert to the United States, there was a small but vocal group who called him a Communist and a radical and opposed his entry. When Albert and Elsa arrived in New York, they were quickly whisked away to their new home in Princeton, New Jersey.

Albert was now beginning a new life and career in the United States as part of the Advanced Institute for Study, but the media attention never stopped. Helen Dukas said, "…living with Professor Einstein, I was accustomed to things turning into a circus wherever he went."

One day soon after the Einsteins arrived in Princeton, a reporter, Carl Peterson, saw "coming towards me a bulky gentleman with wildly flowing hair. Then it dawned on me that it was Einstein." Before Peterson knew it, Einstein had disappeared. Peterson realized that Einstein had probably gone into a Woolworth's store, so he rushed into the store to inquire if a man with shaggy hair had been shopping there. The clerk said yes. That's how Peterson learned that Einstein's first act in Princeton was to purchase a comb. In no time, Peterson wrote an article about Einstein and the comb. It was picked up by newspapers all over the world.

Despite all the fuss and attention he received, when Albert first saw his office at Princeton and was asked what equipment he needed, he simply said: "A desk or table, a chair, paper, and pencil. Oh yes, and a large wastebasket...so I can throw away all my mistakes." Albert and Elsa soon felt comfortable in Princeton. Elsa enjoyed the parklike setting of the city, while Albert enjoyed chatting with local children, riding his bicycle, and taking walks. He always walked alone to his office at the university, absorbed in his thoughts.

Albert enjoyed riding his bicycle.

Although Albert liked living and working in Princeton, he resented institute director Flexner's interference. Flexner wanted to control everything. He'd been handling all of Albert's mail, and when an invitation arrived inviting the Einsteins to the White House, Flexner refused the invitation. Flexner said that the publicity would be damaging to both Albert and the institute. Albert was furious when he found out what Flexner had done and threatened to leave the institute unless he stopped meddling in his affairs. Flexner never bothered him again. In January, Albert and Elsa had an enjoyable dinner with President Roosevelt at the White House and stayed overnight.

In late spring 1934, Elsa learned that her eldest daughter, Ilse, was gravely ill with cancer. Ilse was living with her sister Margot in Paris, and Elsa decided to return to Europe so she could to be with her daughter. It

Franklin D. Roosevelt

Franklin Delano Roosevelt (1882–1945) became president of the United States in 1932 during the Depression, a terrible economic crisis. He was popular for the many social and economic reforms he sponsored, and was elected four times to the presidency. He guided the United States through World War II but died before the war's end.

was too risky for Albert to go, so he stayed behind in Princeton.

Elsa was also concerned about Albert's papers and books. Margot, aided by the underground, a secret group of people who opposed the Nazi government, had smuggled them out of Germany. But with Europe on the brink of war, Elsa still worried about the safety of the documents. Soon after Elsa arrived in Paris, Ilse died. Elsa was shattered. As she prepared

Albert and Elsa lived in this house at 112 Mercer Street in Princeton.

to return to America with Margot, Elsa filled several trunks and cases with Albert's books and papers. On the ship back to the United States, Elsa begged Andrew Blackwood, a Presbyterian minister and friend, to declare, or claim, Albert's paper and books as his own in case the customs officials seized them when they saw that the trunks belonged to Einstein. The United States still had diplomatic relations with Germany, and Albert was considered a criminal by the German government. Elsa feared any publicity about the materials might cause an international incident. Andrew Blackwood agreed to write on his customs form that he had "material acquired in Europe for scholarly purposes." It was a truthful if vague statement, and Albert's material arrived safely in the United States.

That summer, Albert continued to work on his unified theory. To help him relax, Albert loved to sail—although he knew little about navigation or how to maneuver a boat in a storm. He had sailed since his days as a student in Zurich but he never learned how to swim. He also refused to carry charts or life preservers. His friend Leon Watters said that despite this, Albert had "a good sense of direction and never looked at a compass. He could forecast a storm with uncanny accuracy and had no fear of rough weather even though he had to be towed several times when his masts were blown down."

Elsa and Albert were also busy that summer moving into a house at 112 Mercer Street in Princeton. It was a white, two-story house in a quiet neighborhood. On the second floor, the Einsteins installed a huge picture window in Albert's new study. From his window, he had a broad view of parkland. Albert spent many happy hours in that room, deep in his thoughts and work.

But soon after they moved in, Elsa discovered she had a serious heart and kidney condition. When she became gravely ill, Albert spent hours at her bedside, reading and talking to her. Albert had often been so busy with his work that he hadn't spent much time with Elsa, but at the end of her life, Elsa said: "He went around miserable and depressed. I never thought he was so attached to me." Elsa died in December 1936.

Elsa was a devoted wife to Albert, despite his absentminded and often aloof ways.

Three generations of Einsteins sit together: Hans Albert, his son Bernard, and Albert.

Some people felt Albert had always taken Elsa for granted and was often cool and distant toward her. Many who knew him well felt that Albert had a formal relationship with everyone—especially with those who were closest to him. Thomas Bucky, who continued a friendship with Albert for many years, said, "I couldn't describe his attitude to his wife or son Hans Albert as cool. He had a shy attitude toward everybody. He was gentle, considerate of others, and the opposite of pompous. But I never heard even a close friend call him by his first name. When someone did treat him with undue familiarity, he would shrink back."

After Elsa's death, Albert continued his scientific research. As the situation in Europe worsened, he also became increasingly involved in helping people leave Germany, but he decided to keep his efforts quiet. He feared that taking a more public position might do harm to Jews stranded in Nazi Germany. During this time, many friends and colleagues visited Einstein, and an endless stream of people asked for his help for different causes. He continued to support people of every race or group who were discriminated against. He once

Kristallnacht

On November 9, 1937, storm troopers in Germany seized Jewish property, murdered Jews, and ransacked synagogues and Jewish stores and homes. It was a night that would become known as Kristallnacht ("Crystal Night") because of the countless windows shattered. This event caused many people to realize for the first time that Europe's Jews were in grave danger and that Hitler was a threat to all of Europe.

invited renowned African-American singer Marian Anderson to stay at his home when she was refused a room at a Princeton hotel after performing at a concert. They remained friends for the rest of his life.

His younger son, Eduard, was now under full-time psychiatric care and was still living in Zurich. Hans Albert, his older son. also lived in Zurich with his wife and children. In 1937, Hans Albert and his family came to visit Albert in New Jersey. Eduard could not come because U.S. law forbade entry to any mentally ill person. Hans Albert and his family had a wonderful visit with Albert. Their relationship was closer and more relaxed now, a contrast to their earlier thorny relationship. Hans Albert soon settled in the United States with his family.

Hans Albert moved to the United States with his family before World War II began.

chapter 15

War and the Bomb

In 1939, Benito Mussolini, the dictator of Italy, began to adopt many of the same anti-Semitic policies as the Nazis in Germany. Albert's sister, Maja, who lived in Florence, Italy, left to join Albert in Princeton. Albert, who had always felt close to Maja, was delighted to have her live with him. By this time, Albert was spending much of his time helping friends, relatives, and even strangers escape from Nazi-occupied territory.

In the summer of 1939, scientists Leo Szilard and Eugene Wigner approached Einstein. They were concerned that the Germans might be building an atom bomb. If Germany succeeded in developing the bomb, it would give them enormous power to threaten Europe and the entire world. Albert agreed to sign a letter drafted by Szilard strongly urging President Roosevelt to take action. In 1940, Einstein wrote a second letter to the president. Roosevelt was impressed with Einstein's letters. They helped set in motion the creation of The Manhattan Project, a secret U.S. mission to create an atom bomb. Writing the letters to Roosevelt must have been difficult for Einstein, who always abhorred war.

ATOM

An atom is a tiny particle that is a building block for matter. It consists of a nucleus at its center and electrons moving around it.

He never stopped worrying about the results of creating such a powerful and deadly weapon.

Nevertheless, the threat from Germany, as he and many others saw it at the time, was so great that drastic measures had to be taken.

On September 1, 1939, German tanks invaded Poland, and within a few days, France and England joined the war against Germany. Hitler continued his march across Europe by invading Denmark, Norway, Holland, Belgium, and Luxembourg in the spring and summer of 1940. By late 1940, France had surrendered to the Nazis. Britain stood alone against the Nazis in Europe. While the Nazis were invading Europe, Albert, Margot, and Helen Dukas became U.S. citizens in a ceremony in Trenton, New Jersey.

On December 7, 1941, Japanese warplanes made

The Manhattan Project

"Manhattan Project" is the code name for a U.S. effort headed by J. Robert Oppenheimer to produce an atom bomb before the Germans. The project was based in New Mexico and lasted four years. (1942–1946). It produced scientific breakthroughs through a cooperative approach between civilians, military officials, and scientists. The project created the two bombs that were dropped on Japan in 1945. The bombing ended World War II, but debate over this action and how to use atomic energy continues to this day.

a surprise attack on the U.S. Naval base in Hawaii's Pearl Harbor. The United States immediately entered the war against Japan and Germany as work continued on the Manhattan Project. Einstein was never asked to work on the project, but he did contribute to the war effort by

Albert, his stepdaughter Margot, and his secretary Helen Dukas make the pledge of allegiance to the United States to become U.S. citizens.

working for the U.S. Navy's Bureau of Ordinance. He rated and made suggestions about weapons at an early stage in their development. In some ways, this job was like his work at the patent office so many years before.

Throughout these war years, FBI Director J. Edgar Hoover kept secret files detailing the history and activities of many people he considered suspicious, including Einstein. Albert didn't know about the FBI file, but he suspected he was being shut out of scientific activity on atomic energy.

He wrote to a friend: "I have become a lonely old fellow. A kind of patriarch figure who is known chiefly because he does not wear socks and displayed on various

FBI

FBI stands for the Federal Bureau of Investigation, a U.S. governmental agency that investigates crimes involving federal law.

> ## "I have become a lonely old fellow."
> —Albert Einstein

occasions an oddity." Many scientists such as Niels Bohr, who did become part of the atomic research project, escaped from war-ravaged Europe. Some escaped at what seemed like the very last moment under harrowing conditions.

As the war continued, Albert heard more about the atrocities the Nazis were committing, especially the state-ordered killing of European Jews. He tried to find ways to help as many people as possible escape from the Nazis. He was devastated to learn that members of his own family had been killed along with countless other innocent victims. Roberto Einstein's wife and two daughters were murdered by the Nazis. Roberto, the son of Albert's beloved Uncle Jakob, was so shattered by the events, he committed suicide a year later.

In 1945, President Roosevelt died,

Although Albert supported the Allied war movement, the fighting conditions around the world made him worry about the future, especially after the United States dropped the deadly atom bomb on Hiroshima.

Einstein and the Bomb

Einstein was never directly involved in the Manhattan Project for a few reasons. First, FBI director J. Edgar Hoover, considered Albert a suspicious person and a Communist sympathizer, and kept a thick FBI file on him. Second, the work on the bomb dealt mainly with nuclear engineering and nuclear physics, which were not Albert's areas of scientific expertise. In addition, Albert was 63 years old and not in the best of health.

and Harry Truman took his place as president of the United States. After years of bitter fighting and the loss of millions of people on both sides, Germany was finally defeated. On May 7, 1945, Germany surrendered unconditionally. Although the war in Europe was over, the war with Japan was not. President Truman wanted to end that war quickly, and he made a decision that would change the world forever. He ordered the first atom bomb to be dropped on the Japanese city of Hiroshima on August 6, 1945.

The bomb killed 70,000 Japanese civilians instantly, and many more died from injuries not long after. The first bomb was followed three days later by a second. Albert was vacationing with Helen Dukas at Saranac Lake, New York, when the news came over the radio that an atomic bomb had been dropped. He was stunned. He understood why the United States had decided to drop the bomb, and yet he feared for the future now that

nuclear power had been unleashed. He worried that there would be a proliferation of bombs that could endanger the stability and safety of the world. For the rest of his life he would speak out about the dangers of nuclear weapons.

"The atom bomb was no 'great decision.' It was merely another powerful weapon in the arsenal of righteousness."

—President Harry Truman

This devastation is the result of the U.S. nuclear attack on Hiroshima, Japan. Dropping the bomb did shorten the duration of World War II, but many people died in the terrible explosion and its after-effects.

16

Last Years

After the war, Albert continued to work on his unified theory, but he was never able to formulate it. Albert's life was now filled with visitors, scientific work, a huge correspondence, and his political interests.

One of the key issues that continued to interest him was the future of Palestine. The British, who had governed the area for many years, were now debating its future. As the devastation of the Jewish population in Europe became clear, there was further incentive to help the remaining Jews find a sanctuary outside Europe. Palestine was a natural choice because of its long historic bonds to the Jewish people. But the Arab people had also lived there for centuries. Both groups had strong claims to the land.

Albert continued to speak out about the future of Palestine. He believed the land could be shared by the Arabs and Jews. Not everyone agreed with Albert, but he felt that there was merit in the claims of both

Albert loved to relax in his study with friends. Here, he sits with his stepdaughter Margot, a friend, and a playful dog.

sides. His greatest desire was for the two groups to live together cooperatively.

Albert also took a stand on other political issues. He spoke out against the terrible conditions in which black people lived in the American South, and discussed how important it was for Russia and the United States to cooperate, especially with the availability of nuclear weapons. As he continued to speak out on political and social issues, the FBI continued to take note.

McCarthyism

Joe McCarthy (1909–1957) was a Republican senator who sought out to suppress Communism— the belief that private property should be relinquished for the common good, a Russian political ideal of the time. Members of the Communist Party were sought out and questioned using information turned over by the FBI and collected from citizens. McCarthy's investigations and "blacklists" destroyed the careers of many innocent people. Eventually, McCarthy was defeated and his activities stopped by courageous members of Congress and the media.

The fear of Communism was rampant in the United States, and many people were suffering the consequences.

By April 1947, Albert's beloved sister, Maja, suffered a stroke. Each evening, Albert would sit by his sister's bedside and read to her. Albert learned that his ex-wife Mileva was also unwell, and that his son Eduard needed further care and periods of time in the hospital. Many of Albert's old friends were dying or had recently died, and he missed them. They had been a special part of his life and work.

Although he officially retired from the Institute for

Advanced Study in 1947, Einstein still kept his office and worked on his unified theory a few times a week. Albert always still enjoyed speaking with neighborhood children. He liked their directness and openness to new ideas. In many ways, he credited his own childlike curiosity and openness to new ways of thinking with helping him formulate his scientific ideas. He said, "How did it come to pass that I was the one to develop the theory of relativity? The reason I think is that a normal adult never stops to think about problems of space and time. These are things which he has thought of as a child." Einstein also once declared that people know all the physics they need to know by the age of three. He believed that children have a natural and instinctive understanding of how

Even after his health problems began, Albert loved his solitary walk to work, which allowed him to continue reflecting on new ideas.

things work. He was always fascinated by how children think.

On August 4, 1948, Mileva suffered a stroke and died in Switzerland. Albert arranged for a guardian to protect his son Eduard's interests, since Eduard was often confined to a mental institution.

Albert himself soon became ill and required surgery. It was discovered that he had a large aneurysm, a ballooning of his main artery, the aorta. If it burst, it would prove fatal. The surgeons decided not to operate and encouraged Albert to rest. Albert maintained his sense of humor. On his way home from the hospital, after being hounded by photographers, he playfully stuck out his tongue. The resulting picture was printed in newspapers everywhere.

As Albert's 70th birthday approached in 1949, the officials at Princeton University decided to hold a public celebration. They invited many distinguished scientists to speak at the event. It was a special milestone for Einstein, but a difficult time,

Albert was a popular and approachable professor at Princeton. Despite his elite reputation, many students looked upon him as a kindly uncle.

After surgery, Albert proves that his sense of humor is intact.

too. Maja was seriously ill, and he wasn't well himself. His scientific work wasn't progressing in the way he had hoped, despite years of work, and he felt left out of the mainstream of scientific thought. He also worried about the continued rise of McCarthyism and the destructive investigations of innocent people. Einstein was concerned that the United States was heading toward Fascism.

In June 1951, Maja died. Albert missed her terribly, but he still tried to keep active. He was becoming weaker, but he continued to walk to his old office at the institute in all weather.

Then, in 1952, a few days after his friend President Chaim Weizmann of Israel died, Albert was offered the presidency of Israel. He was touched but knew he had to decline. He wrote: "All my life I have dealt with objective matters. Hence, I lack both a natural aptitude and the experience to deal properly with people and exercise official functions. For these reasons alone, I should be unsuited to fulfill the duties of high office, even if advancing age was not making increasing inroads on my strength."

The last few years of Albert's life were racked by illness and weakness, although he rarely complained. He still actively corresponded with colleagues, advocated for peace, and pursued his

Both Albert and his friend David Ben-Gurion played a crucial role in founding the state of Israel.

work on the unified field theory, which he never ceased to believe was possible.

One of his last acts was working with philosopher Bertrand Russell to establish a conference to discuss the possible effects of atomic weapons on the world and to encourage governments "to find peaceful means for the settlement of all matters of dispute between them." The conference, known as the Pugwash Conference, has continued to this day.

Albert's sanctuary was his study, where he devoted hours to developing the unified field theory which he believed would be his greatest discovery.

On April 12, 1955, Albert collapsed at home. Hans Albert flew in from California to be with his father. Margot also visited him there. Albert recovered somewhat and requested a pen and paper while in the hospital. He scribbled equations, wrote notes, and spoke to Margot and Helen Dukas. But he knew he was dying. The aneurysm he had been living with had finally burst. On April 18, 1955, Albert Einstein died. He was 76 years old.

Margot wrote: "As fearless as he had been all his life so he faced death humbly and quietly. He left the world without sentimentality and regrets."

chapter 17

Still the Most Famous Scientist in the World

Years after his death, the world is still fascinated with Albert Einstein. In 2000, *Time* magazine chose him as Person of the Century. What is it about Albert Einstein that still intrigues us?

Perhaps we are fascinated with him because his personality and life were full of conflict, contrast, humor, perseverance, failure, and achievement, just like ours.

When he was young, he had temper tantrums that terrified his family, but he could also play contentedly for hours.

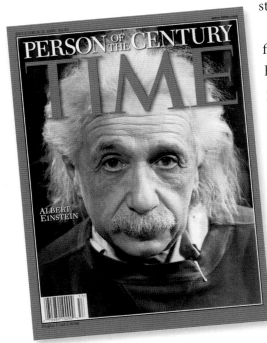

Albert's influence is as powerful today as it was during his lifetime, making him an ideal choice as *Time* magazine's "Person of the Century."

He resented being forced to play the violin, but by the time he was a teenager, he discovered the violin and loved playing. As a student, he hated being compelled to memorize, but throughout his life, he loved learning.

He despised war and militarism, but he came to believe that some wars and some enemies are so menacing, they must be fought and defeated.

He was a brilliant thinker who was sometimes so absent-minded that he lost his keys or his way home. He loved the logic and orderliness of science, yet he didn't care what he wore. He didn't even mind that his papers and books were piled high or that his office was dusty and in disorder.

He helped countless people, some he never knew, escape the horrors of Nazi Germany, but at times he was so absorbed in his work that he neglected his own family.

He signed anti-war documents in Germany when few people dared to protest World War I. He wrote letters to President Roosevelt, which helped set in motion the creation of an atom bomb that would be used to end World War II. For the rest of his life, he cautioned the world about misusing this terrible new weapon.

He had no patience for fools and fearlessly spoke his mind despite criticism. He had a wonderful sense of humor and great patience for children.

He was one of the world's first celebrities. He enjoyed being with friends and family. He also loved being alone to think and work.

Perhaps we are intrigued by him because, as James Gleick wrote in *Time* magazine: "The scientific touchstones of our age-the bomb, space travel, electronics, all bear his fingerprints."

Dr. Michael M. Shara said: "We would not understand the expansion of the universe or how matter behaves on the large scale in the universe, were it not for General Relativity." Shara also notes there were more changes in technology in the 20th century than in the previous two thousand years. He attributes much of that to Einstein's work. He says that even the biological revolution can be traced to Einstein's work on the existence and size of molecules and that his work on Brownian motion is "fundamental to our knowledge of molecules." Even the computer chip and lasers can be linked to Einstein's explanation of the photoelectric effect.

Thoughtful and absent-minded, charismatic and reserved, Einstein was a man full of contrasts.

The year 2005 marks the centennial of that amazing year 1905, when Einstein published five papers that revolutionized science. Germany, the country of Einstein's birth, has launched a year of celebrations to mark the occasion. Einstein would have probably found it ironic that the country whose educational system he despised, whose citizenship he renounced, and whose political system he denounced during the Nazi era, would honor him in this way. He would have probably been delighted, too, for the Germany of today is a different country than the Germany of the 1930s. Today Germany is a democracy, and Einstein's beliefs and work are valued. In launching the 2005 "Einstein Year", German chancellor Gerhard Schroeder said: "Despite being exposed to increasing anti-Semitic attacks, Einstein always fought against the strengthening of Nazism and for the strengthening of democracy." Chancellor Schroeder called on intellectuals and scientists today to follow his example and "play a greater role in political debate and involve themselves in the challenges facing our society."

Throughout his life, Einstein was not only a man of great scientific accomplishments, but a great humanitarian who spoke out against tyranny and injustice wherever he found it. He was a fascinating and complex person who never stopped questioning and learning. He was a brilliant and original thinker, but he knew he had unlocked only part of the puzzle of how the universe worked. His ideas continue to influence out lives and the world.

Events in the Life of Albert Einstein

March 14, 1879
Albert Einstein is born in Ulm, Germany.

October 1896–1900
Albert studies at the Swiss Polytechnic Institute.

1905
Albert publishes five revolutionary scientific papers and receives his Ph.D. from Zurich University.

December 29, 1894
Albert moves to Italy to join his family.

1902
Albert is appointed technical expert third class at patent office in Bern, Switzerland.

1888
Albert enrolls in the Luitpold Gymnasium.

1895
Albert enrolls in school in Aarau, Switzerland.

1903
Albert and Mileva Maric marry in Bern.

1908
Albert is appointed a lecturer at Bern University.

1909
Albert resigns from the patent office and takes a position as associate Professor in Physics at Zurich University.

1901
Albert becomes a Swiss citizen.

1932
Albert and Elsa move to Princeton, New Jersey.

1911
Albert and Mileva move to Prague.

April 18, 1955
Albert Einstein dies in Princeton.

1914
Albert is appointed a professor at University of Berlin. Mileva returns to Zurich with Hans Albert and Eduard.

1939
World War II begins in Europe.

1922
Albert wins the 1921 Nobel Prize.

1916
Albert publishes a paper on the General Theory of Relativity.

1919
Albert divorces Mileva and marries his cousin Elsa. Eddington's expedition confirms Einstein's theory that light bends.

1936
Elsa Einstein dies.

1912
Albert returns to teach at the Swiss Polytechnic Institute.

1921
The Einsteins visit the United States with Chaim Weizmann.

Bibliography

Bernstein, Jeremy. EINSTEIN. New York: Penguin, 1973.

Bondi, Hermann. RELATIVITY AND COMMON SENSE. New York: Anchor Books, 1964.

Brian, Denis. EINSTEIN. A LIFE . New York: John Wiley & Sons, Inc., 1996.

Bucky, Peter A. with Allen G. Weakland. THE PRIVATE ALBERT EINSTEIN. Kansas City: Andrews & McMeel, 1992.

Calaprice, Alice. THE EXPANDED QUOTABLE EINSTEIN. New Jersey: The Princeton University Press, 2000.

Clark, Ronald W. EINSTEIN THE LIFE AND TIMES. New York: World Publishing Co., 1971.

Folsing, Albrecht. ALBERT EINSTEIN. New York: Viking, 1997.

Frank, Philipp. EINSTEIN: HIS LIFE AND TIMES. translated by George Rosen. New York: Knopf, 1947.

Gardner, Howard. CREATING MINDS. New York: HarperCollins, 1993.

Goldsmith, Donald with Robert Libbon. THE ULTIMATE EINSTEIN. New York: Simon & Schuster, 1997.

Hoffmann, Banesh with Helen Dukas. ALBERT EINSTEIN CREATOR AND REBEL. New York: Viking, 1972.

Levenson, Thomas. EINSTEIN IN BERLIN. New York: Bantam, 2003.

McPherson, Stephanie Sammartino. ORDINARY GENIUS. Minneapolis: Lerner, 1995.

Overbye, Dennis. EINSTEIN IN LOVE. New York: Penguin, 2000.

Pais, Abraham, SUBTLE IS THE LORD...THE SCIENCE AND LIFE OF ALBERT EINSTEIN, New York: Oxford University Press, 1982.

Pais, Abraham. EINSTEIN LIVED HERE. New York: Oxford University Press, 1994.

Parker, Barry. EINSTEIN THE PASSIONS OF A SCIENTIST. New York: Prometheus Books, 2003.

Pyenson, Lewis. THE YOUNG EINSTEIN. Boston: Adam Hilger, 1985.

Swisher, Clarice. THE IMPORTANCE OF ALBERT EINSTEIN. San Diego: Lucent Books, 1994.

White, Michael and Gribbin, John. EINSTEIN A LIFE IN SCIENCE. New York: Simon and Schuster, 1993.

Wishinsky, Frieda. WHAT'S THE MATTER WITH ALBERT? Toronto: Maple Tree Press, 2002.

Wolfson, Richard. SIMPLY EINSTEIN. New York: W.W. Norton & Company, 2003.

Works Cited

Note: Spelling and punctuation have been modernized for easier reading.

"Much too fat..." on p. 9: EINSTEIN A LIFE p.1.

"When I was between..." on p. 10: SUBTLE IS THE LORD...THE LIFE AND GENIUS OF ALBERT EINSTEIN p. 36.

"Where are the wheels?" on p. 10: EINSTEIN A LIFE p.1.

"A sound skull..." on p. 14: EINSTEIN A LIFE p.3.

"I can still..." on p. 15: ALBERT EINSTEIN p.14.

"Albert got his grades..." on p. 17: ALBERT EINSTEIN p.16

"The worst thing..." on p.19: EINSTEIN THE LIFE AND TIMES p.13

"When we bag..." on p.20: EINSTEIN THE PASSIONS OF A SCIENTIST p.25

"Persistence and tenacity..." on p.20: EINSTEIN THE PASSIONS OF A SCIENTIST p. 25

"In all those years..." on p. 21: SUBTLE IS THE LORD... p.38

"He showed a particular..." on p.21: EINSTEIN THE LIFE AND TIMES p. 15

"Soon the flight..." on p.23: EINSTEIN THE LIFE AND TIMES p. 16

"Constantly searched..." on p.24: EINSTEIN A LIFE p.6

"I believe on the whole..." on p. 24: THE EXPANDED QUOTABLE EINSTEIN p.14

"You sit there..." on p. 27: EINSTEIN A LIFE p.7

"The people of Northern..." on p. 27: ALBERT EINSTEIN p.34

"...an unforgettable oasis..." on p.29: EINSTEIN A LIFE p. 9

"This school has left..." on p.30: SUBTLE IS THE LORD p. 40

"One student, by the name of..." on p. 30: EINSTEIN THE PASSIONS OF A SCIENTIST p.50

"My desires have also..." on p. 30: ALBERT EINSTEIN p.45

"Sure of himself..." on p 31: EINSTEIN A LIFE p.11

"Einstein will be..." on p. 33: EINSTEIN THE PASSIONS OF A SCIENTIST p.58

"When I was a very..." on p. 34: EINSTEIN

For Further Study

The Albert Einstein archives at the Hebrew University in Jerusalem, Israel, is an excellent source of Einstein information. Albert Einstein willed all his papers to the Hebrew University. (www.albert-einstein.org/)

The American Institute of Physics is a good site for information and links on Einstein and his work. (www.aip.org/history/Einstein/)

The American Museum of Natural History's outstanding exhibit on Albert Einstein, curated by Dr. Michael M. Shara, also provides an outstanding Web site. (www.amnh.org/exhibits/einstein/index.php)

Index

Acknowledgments

My special thanks to Dr. Michael M. Shara who was so generous with his time and provided helpful
and specific comments on the manuscript. The Einstein exhibition Dr. Shara curated for the
American Museum of Natural History was an inspiration and I thank all those who assisted in put-
ting it together. My thanks to my wonderful agents, Lynn and David Bennett and Marie Campbell of
TLA, for their continued support and wise counsel. Warm thanks to my editor Beth Hester for her
good humor and excellent suggestions. Beth helped make it a pleasure to work on this project. I am
most grateful to three special friends and fellow authors, Sharon Siamon, Kathy Guttman, and Anne
Dublin for their friendship and advice. Most of all my thanks to my husband Dr. Bill Wishinsky,
who not only helped clarify the science but whose perceptive editorial skills continue to amaze me.

Picture Credits

About the Author

Frieda Wishinsky is the international award winning author of more than 30 trade and educational books. Her books have earned critical acclaim and have been reviewed in magazines and newspapers around the world, including *The New York Times, The London Times,* and *The Observer.* They have been translated into many languages, including French, Dutch, Danish, Swedish, Spanish, and Catalan.

Frieda lives in Toronto, Ontario, with her family and enjoys speaking at schools, libraries, and conferences in Canada, the United States, and the United Kingdom.

Other DK Biographies you may enjoy:

DK Biography: *Harry Houdini*
by Vicki Cobb
ISBN 0-7566-1245-4 paperback
ISBN 0-7566-1246-2 hardcover

DK Biography: *Abraham Lincoln*
by Tanya Lee Stone
ISBN 0-7566-0341-2 paperback
ISBN 0-7566-0490-7 hardcover

DK Biography: *George Washington*
by Lenny Hort
ISBN 0-7566-0835-X paperback
ISBN 0-7566-0832-5 hardcover

DK Biography: *Anne Frank*
by Kem Knapp Sawyer
ISBN 0-7566-0341-2 paperback
ISBN 0-7566-0490-7 hardcover

DK Biography: *Martin Luther King, Jr.*
by Amy Pastan
ISBN 0-7566-0342-0 paperback
ISBN 0-7566-0491-5 hardcover

DK Biography: *Helen Keller*
by Leslie Garrett
ISBN 0-7566-0339-0 paperback
ISBN 0-7566-0488-5 hardcover

DK Biography: *John F. Kennedy*
by Howard S. Kaplan
ISBN 0-7566-0340-4 paperback
ISBN 0-7566-0489-3 hardcover

Look what the critics are saying about DK Biography!

"…highly readable, worthwhile overviews for young people…"—*Booklist*

"This new series from the inimitable DK Publishing brings together the usual brilliant photography with a historian's approach to biography subjects."
—*Ingram Library Services*